The Sins of Education

of

Education

A Transformational Blueprint

Ratanjit S Sondhe
&
Gurdip Hari

ISBN: 978-1-968953-00-3

Library of Congress Control Number: 2025942643

First Trade Paperback Edition

Published in USA by:
Bliss in Unity
18 Indiana, Irvine, CA 92606, USA

Published in India by:
Bliss in Unity
73, Sector 2, Chandigarh, India

Typeset in Minion Pro by Sanjay Mishra, Mohali, India

For inquiries, email: info@blissinunity.com
(Emails to the authors may also be directed to this address)

Website: https://blissinunity.com

Who This Book Is For ...

This book is for the many who shape the way,
For parents who nurture with love's quiet might,
For teachers who kindle the fire of insight,
For policymakers who dare to dream anew,
For reformers who labor to build what is true.

It is for the young, with open minds and songs unsung,
The architects of futures yet to be spun.
You hold the power to shift life's streams,
Through your vision, bold and free,
A better world is yet to be.

And it is for every soul who believes
That learning can heal, and wisdom redeems.

Grasp the power that today bestows,
Break the limits that the old world knows.
Shine your light, let your spirits soar,
Together, we are the future, and so much more.

Foreword

By Gurdip Hari

Educator | Author | Founder, Healthy-Mind International School

L et me begin with a story—a thread of serendipity that wove my soul into this sacred work of global educational reform.

It was the winter of 2016, and I found myself in Chandigarh—one of India's most soul-stirring cities—to personally deliver a wedding invitation for my daughter, Jasmin. The recipient was Khushwant Singh, a brilliant young author whose works had already captured hearts and minds across the country. After an hour of deep, reflective conversation, he rose quietly, disappeared into his study, and returned with a book pressed close to his heart. "This," he said, placing it gently in my hands, "is your twin brother in the United States."

The book was *Mending Souls*—the biography of Indian-American entrepreneur Ratanjit S. Sondhe. "I lived with him for four months in his sprawling estate in Cleveland while writing this," Khushwant shared. "And after listening to you for the past hour, I can say this without a shadow of doubt—you and he are identical twins, not by birth, but by soul. You share the same worldview, the same spiritual compass, and a luminous vision of selfless service. Both of you live by the timeless truth of Oneness and embody the sacred mindset of 'What am I here to give?'—transforming consciousness into contribution, vision into service, and success into a soulful offering."

Then, with quiet certainty, he added, "I will connect you both—and perhaps, something divine will unfold, something that may bless the world."

True to his word, Khushwant connected us. And what unfolded was nothing short of divine orchestration. Ratanjit and I spoke, met, and discovered a resonance so deep it felt predestined—as if two flames from the same eternal fire had found each other once more. When he completed his manuscript for *The Sins of Education*, he placed it in my hands and said, "Now it is yours to refine, elevate, and complete."

And so, with reverence and resolve, I took it forward. I call this book *His Soul and My Body*—a co-creation born of spiritual kinship, a shared longing to awaken the sacred within education. Two voices. One essence. A united offering to help heal one of the world's deepest wounds.

There are books that pass through the mind, and there are books that pass through the soul—gently stirring something ancient, something eternal, something true. The *Sins of Education* is one such book.

This is not a book of criticism, but of awakening. It is not simply an argument for change, but a revelation—a remembering of what education was always meant to be: not a mechanical preparation for survival, but a sacred pilgrimage toward self-realization, wisdom, and purpose.

In these pages, we explore how the modern education system—despite its outward advancements—has silently abandoned its soul. In the pursuit of grades, we have forgotten grace. In the race for achievement, we have lost alignment. And yet, this book does not merely dwell in critique. It rises—with poetic power and piercing clarity—into a vision of what could be, and more importantly, what already is beginning to bloom.

As founder of Healthy-Mind International School, I have witnessed firsthand the transformative power of reimagined education. I have seen children who once feared school now walk through its doors with joy. I have seen families healed, spirits awakened, talents unleashed—all because we dared to place the soul back at the center of learning.

This book weaves together not only insight and inspiration, but also living stories of transformation. It offers a new blueprint for education—one rooted in self-knowledge, inner confidence, service, and the sacred collaboration between pupil, parent, and teacher. It is both a call to action and a compass for those who are ready to lead education into a more conscious, compassionate, and awakened future.

If you are an educator, a parent, a student, or a seeker—know that this book is for you. Let it not just change your mind, but open your heart. Let it awaken in you the highest question of all: What am I here to give?

For when education is guided by this question, it does not merely inform—it transforms. And in doing so, it holds the power to heal not only individuals, but the world.

Gurdip Hari
Educator | Author | Founder, Healthy-Mind International School

Table of Contents

An Approach for Reading this Book

This book is an invitation—a call to awaken, to question, and to rediscover the true essence of education. It is not merely a collection of insights but a portal to transformation—a path that may challenge your deepest beliefs, stretch your perceptions, and shift the very way you think, act, and live.

The education explored in these pages is not confined to the walls of schools, colleges, or universities. It is the great unfolding of life itself—a force that shapes us, moment by moment, through every experience, encounter, and lesson. It is found in the whispers of wisdom passed down through generations, in the silent teachings of hardship and triumph, in the questions that stir within us long after the textbooks are closed. It is the ceaseless evolution of the soul, a journey without end, an awakening without boundaries.

The key to this journey is not merely acquiring knowledge but embracing the art of discovery—of yourself, of others, of the universe in which you exist. The revelations within this book may challenge the foundations upon which your life has been built—the traditions you were raised with, the lessons you were taught, and the framework through which you have come to understand success, identity, and purpose. But growth is born not from certainty, but from openness.

An open mind is a gateway to boundless possibilities—both seen and unseen, both carefully planned and divinely unexpected. As you read, you may find yourself confronted by emotions that stir deep within, moments of resonance that feel like long-forgotten truths reawakened. Stay with them. Every challenge to your perspective is an invitation to expansion; every discomfort is the threshold of transformation. For the ideas woven through these pages do not merely seek to inform, but to awaken—to remind you of who you truly are.

The highest purpose of education is to help us live fully—to uncover our unique potential, refine it to its greatest expression, and grasp the deeper meaning of the life we have been given. True education does not teach us merely to survive; it teaches us to illuminate, to create, to give. It is through this awareness that we become forces of change—shaping not only our own destiny but leaving an indelible mark upon the world, enriching the lives of others, uplifting society, and harmonizing with the natural order of existence.

A gentle note as you embark on this journey: you may encounter certain ideas echoed and interwoven throughout these pages. This repetition is intentional—meant to reinforce and immerse you in the core truths that hold the power to transform not just your educational path, but the very fabric of your life's journey.

As you move through each chapter, let the insights settle within you. Allow them to resonate, expand, and take root in your consciousness. I encourage you to revisit these words, not just once, but many times, for true understanding is not found in mere reading—it is activated through reflection, experience, and embodiment.

My deepest hope is that these pages do not simply inspire you, but ignite a renewed sense of purpose—one that fuels your quest to understand life, the universe, and your irreplaceable place within it.

Remember: You are a masterpiece. A rare and luminous gift. A treasure beyond measure.

Let your light shine—not as a flicker, but as a beacon, illuminating the world with the full brilliance of your being.

Prelude: The Sacred Architecture Behind This Journey

There are journeys that unfold across the landscapes of the world—and there are journeys that unfold across the infinite landscapes of the soul.

This book, "The Sins of Education," was not composed as a random collection of reflections or critiques. It was shaped upon an ancient, sacred map—drawn from the Fool's Journey of the Tarot's Major Arcana, the mystical ascent of the soul revealed through the Kabbalistic Tree of Life, the timeless teachings imparted by Krishna to Arjuna upon the battlefield of Kurukshetra, and the divine revelation of Oneness unveiled by Guru Nanak, who proclaimed that all human beings are eternal seekers of life—Sikhs, walking the sacred path of self-realization.

The Fool—the seeker numbered zero—symbolizes the pure soul: unburdened by convention, standing at the edge of a mountain, eyes lifted to the sky, trusting the unknown with childlike wonder. Arjuna—the warrior prince—mirrors this same seeker, standing at the brink of battle, torn between doubt and purpose, and guided back to his higher calling by the Divine Charioteer. And the Sikh—the eternal seeker—walks not by creed but by consciousness, remembering what the soul has always known: that life is not a summit to conquer, but a sacred unfolding—a return to our divine wholeness, where every edge is also a beginning.

Through each chapter of this work, you will walk alongside this sacred traveler:

From innocence to awakening,
From entanglement to liberation,
From fragmented knowledge to integrated wisdom,
From isolated ambition to sacred service,

From the confines of worldly education into the vastness of soul mastery.

The chapters mirror not only the outward progression of human learning, but the timeless spiral of inner evolution—passing through the trials of the mind, the tests of the heart, the deaths of old identities, and the rebirths into higher realms of awareness.

This journey echoes the mystical wisdom encoded across cultures—from the hidden paths of Kabbalah, to the spiritual archetypes of the Tarot, to Krishna's eternal guidance for the soul caught between despair and duty, and to Guru Nanak's revelation of Oneness—Ik Onkaar—the foundational truth affirming the shared divine essence of all humanity.

Whether or not you are versed in these ancient systems, know that their sacred current weaves silently through every page you are about to read. Each lesson, each reflection, each transformation is not merely a personal challenge—it is an invitation to align with the universal laws that have guided seekers since the beginning of time.

For those called to a deeper study through their inner voice—for seekers, mystics, educators, and pilgrims of consciousness—a contemplative chart and analysis awaits in the "Invitation to the Sacred Blueprint" and "Appendix." There, the divine architecture is made visible: the parallels between each chapter and these mystical traditions revealed not as rigid structures, but as sacred gateways for reflection, integration, and inner alignment.

This book is a call to remember: Education is not the filling of the mind, but the awakening of the soul. And the true destination is not success, but the divine remembrance of our sacred unity.

Welcome, fellow traveler, to the path your soul has always known.

Introduction

A Mind is a Terrible Thing to Waste

The year was 1972, and the world was introduced to a slogan so poignant, so evocative, that its resonance echoes profoundly even today: "A mind is a terrible thing to waste." More than just a phrase, it was a clarion call to the transformative power of education—a force capable of sculpting lives, communities, and the trajectory of humanity itself. At its core, it was an acknowledgment that the greatest resource any society possesses is not its wealth, its infrastructure, or its technological advancements, but rather, the untapped brilliance within its people.

And yet, as the decades have passed, that once-hopeful mantra has begun to carry a note of quiet lament. The truth of the message remains, but its promise feels increasingly unfulfilled. We continue to build schools, fund universities, and expand access to information, and yet something essential remains missing—something inward, reflective, and sacred.

For education has strayed from cultivating the interior life. It no longer invites contemplation—the spacious stillness in which the mind encounters meaning. It discourages exploration, treating curiosity not as a divine impulse but a distraction from standardized outcomes. And it neglects introspection, the gentle turning inward by which a learner begins to understand the self in relation to the world, to values, to purpose.

Education—once envisioned as the great equalizer, the architect of opportunity, the key to unlocking a more just and enlightened future—now finds itself faltering, not only in America but across the world. Despite unprecedented levels of funding, technological advancements, and the accessibility of knowledge, the modern education system has drifted from its sacred mission.

Rather than liberating minds, it shackles them in bureaucracy, standardization, and the monotony of rote memorization. Instead of igniting curiosity, it extinguishes the spark of inquiry. Instead of cultivating wisdom, it fosters conformity.

No longer preparing individuals for lives of meaning, purpose, and ethical integrity, education too often molds them into cogs in a relentless machine—workers, not thinkers; competitors, not collaborators; achievers, not visionaries. It churns out graduates equipped for economic survival, yet ill-prepared for the deeper complexities of life: ethical dilemmas, emotional resilience, and the timeless quest for meaning. In a world starving for visionaries, we are manufacturing mere technicians.

The American Influence on Global Education

The current stagnation in global education finds its roots, in part, in the homogenization of learning models—many of which trace their lineage to the American experiment in mass education. The United States, once a trailblazer in universal schooling, established the structural blueprint that many nations have since adopted: the twelve-year K–12 sequence, the primacy of standardized testing, and the relentless pursuit of measurable outcomes as proxies for understanding.

From the SAT to China's Gaokao and India's JEE, performance-driven assessments have transformed learning from a sacred journey of inquiry into a high-stakes contest of numbers. In this race for ranks and credentials, the soul of education—the art of wondering, questioning, and becoming—has been eclipsed by a fixation on performance and prestige.

The commodification of knowledge, particularly in the U.S., has elevated diplomas above discernment, creating a global culture where credentials masquerade as competence. Degrees are prized more than wisdom, and institutions, now marketplaces, serve not as sanctuaries for learning but as gatekeepers of economic ascent.

As America surged toward scientific and technological supremacy, its emphasis on STEM education swept across continents. But in that tide, the softer sciences—the humanities, philosophy, ethics, and social reflection—were left behind like ancient artifacts of a bygone era. The disciplines that nurture conscience and cultivate compassion have been overshadowed by algorithms, outputs, and efficiency.

What was once a vision of universal education as a tool for enlightenment has, over time, been reduced to a mechanized system of economic survival. American education—though once a beacon of innovation and opportunity—has now become a global export, shaping schools across Europe, Asia, Africa, and Latin America with the same performance-driven, high-stakes mentality.

The British Influence: Colonial Legacy and Rigid Structures

If the American model spread through cultural dominance and modern aspiration, the British educational system traveled through empire—its impact more historical, hierarchical, and enduring. Rooted in tradition and shaped by centuries of classical instruction, the British model imprinted itself across the globe through colonial rule and the institutions it left behind.

In Commonwealth nations—India, Pakistan, Singapore, South Africa, and across the African continent—the legacy of British education lives on in structured syllabi, examination-driven pedagogy, and a deep reverence for order. The classroom became a theater of compliance, where imagination gave way to memorization, and discipline was prized above dialogue.

Where the American model championed mass access, the British system built walls—subtle yet profound—between classes. It enshrined hierarchy through its division between elite institutions

(Eton, Harrow, Oxford, Cambridge) and the broader machinery of public education, embedding a reverence for prestige that still shapes global perceptions of educational value.

The examination became not just a tool of assessment, but a rite of passage—an instrument of sorting that reduced knowledge to retention and potential to performance. In its most rigid forms, the British system treated students not as gardens to be cultivated but as containers to be filled, measured, and ranked.

Though differing in tone—one brashly egalitarian, the other steeped in tradition—both systems share a tragic symmetry: a tendency to prioritize system over soul. In their pursuit of excellence, both neglected the inner landscape of the learner—the realm of emotion, intuition, morality, and meaning. And in doing so, they helped build a global architecture of education that, while vast in reach, remains incomplete in essence, and increasingly detached from the holistic development of human potential.

The Cost of a Broken System

The consequences of this failure are not merely academic; they are societal, economic, and spiritual. The fractures we see in the world today—divisions, inequities, political corruption, and even war—are not isolated events. They are the inevitable byproducts of an education system that has taught us to survive, but not to thrive; to follow, but not to question; to succeed materially, but not to succeed morally or spiritually.

Our education has instilled ambition, but not ethics; skill, but not self-awareness; knowledge, but not wisdom. It has trained individuals to compete, but not to contribute; to accumulate, but not to awaken.

And so, we are left with a haunting question:

Is education still alive? Or has it become a lifeless institution, a relic of its former promise, devoid of the vitality it once held?

The Promise of Education

Education is not merely a system—it is a sacred promise, a bridge between ignorance and knowledge, between despair and hope, between mediocrity and greatness. At its highest potential, education is not just about learning facts, memorizing data, or passing exams. It is about awakening the mind, expanding one's perception of the world, and unlocking the infinite potential that lies dormant within every individual.

When education is done right, it elevates the individual, strengthens communities, and builds societies capable of justice, innovation, and ethical leadership. In its purest form, education is not a transaction—it is a transformation. It does not merely prepare one for a career; it prepares one for life itself.

The World Development Report of 2018 outlined education's transformative power across four essential dimensions:

Individual/Family	Community/Society
Monetary—Higher earnings, reduced poverty, economic growth.	Nonmonetary—Better health, civic engagement, life satisfaction.

Yet, despite these promises, modern education has become increasingly transactional, reduced to little more than a means to secure employment, climb the social ladder, or amass wealth. It has become a mechanized system designed not to cultivate enlightenment, but to churn out graduates who are optimized for economic productivity.

This narrow, utilitarian approach to education has resulted in a tragic illusion, answering only the question: "What's in it for me?" In doing so, it has lost its higher calling—to shape thoughtful, ethical, and self-aware citizens capable of contributing to a just and harmonious society.

This fixation on survival has birthed a dangerous illusion: that success is measured by titles, wealth, and status. The pursuit of an MBA, for instance, is often framed as a gateway to financial prosperity, reinforcing the notion that an individual's worth is tied to their economic value. This perspective reduces education to a mere investment, where the ultimate return is financial gain rather than intellectual, ethical, or spiritual growth.

But history has shown us that intelligence, without ethical grounding, can be dangerous. As The Wall Street Journal chillingly observed in 2019, "Who do you think committed cybercrimes in 2018 that cost the global economy $500 billion?" The answer? Highly educated individuals.

Education, without a moral foundation, does not uplift—it corrupts. It does not enlighten—it manipulates. It does not lead to progress—it fuels greed, deceit, and exploitation.

This is not the life education was meant to cultivate.

This is not the future we were meant to inherit.

Is Education Dead?

To question whether education is still alive is to confront the unsettling reality of an institution in decline. Philosopher John Dewey famously wrote, "Education is not preparation for life; education is life itself." Yet today's system feels lifeless—sterile, mechanical, devoid of the passion, curiosity, and intellectual vibrancy that once defined it.

Dewey envisioned education as a dynamic, ever-evolving force, tailored to engage students' unique strengths, interests, and life experiences. It was meant to be a living dialogue between teachers, students, families, and society itself—constantly adapting, constantly questioning, constantly expanding the horizons of human understanding.

But today, Dewey's vision has largely been abandoned. Education has become rigid and formulaic, driven not by the pursuit of wisdom but by the pressures of standardized testing, rankings, and economic outcomes. The result? A system that fails in three fundamental ways:

1. **Erroneous Foundations**: Education has been hijacked by self-serving agendas—whether political, economic, or ideological. Instead of fostering free thought, it enforces conformity. Instead of encouraging exploration, it punishes deviation from the norm.

2. **Lack of Universal Truths**: The modern curriculum often ignores fundamental principles that transcend cultural, religious, and national boundaries—principles such as integrity, empathy, self-awareness, and service to others. Instead, it promotes a worldview rooted in competition, fear, and self-interest.

3. **Focus on Employability, Not Growth**: Schools have become factories for producing employable workers, rather than institutions for cultivating deep thinkers, ethical leaders, and compassionate human beings. Graduates may leave with technical proficiency, but many lack the resilience, critical thinking skills, and ethical grounding necessary to navigate life's complexities.

The Sins of Education

Our education system, in its current form, perpetuates a cycle of hollow learning and superficial success. Year after year, it fails to:

- Inspire lifelong curiosity and intellectual engagement.
- Cultivate genuine critical thinking and independent reasoning.
- Recognize and nurture individual talents and passions.
- Unleash the boundless creative and spiritual potential within each student.
- Foster integrity, ethical discernment, and moral responsibility.

- Instill habits essential for true success and holistic well-being.
- Equip individuals with lifelong skills to lead with compassion, confidence, and clarity of purpose.

Instead, it teaches conformity, rewards mediocrity, and upholds a distorted vision of success. It traps us in a mindset of "What's in it for me?" while ignoring the deeper question: "What am I here to give?"

Adding to the complexity, consider the enigma of twins raised in identical environments yet developing divergent values, beliefs, and behaviors. This phenomenon hints at the profound individuality of human learning—shaped not just by external factors but by internal filters unique to each person. Education, therefore, must do more than impart knowledge; it must help individuals uncover their inner compass and understand the forces shaping their character.

This book, "The Sins of Education," seeks to illuminate the flaws in our current system and reimagine a path forward. It is a call to return to education's true purpose: to awaken the mind, nurture the spirit, and prepare individuals to contribute meaningfully to the world. It challenges us to build a system rooted in universal values, fostering not just knowledge but wisdom; not just ambition but empathy; not just survival but flourishing.

We must ask ourselves: What does it mean to truly educate? What does it mean to truly learn?

The answers to these questions do not lie in rigid curricula, standardized tests, or outdated teaching methodologies. They are found in the courage to question, the willingness to evolve, and the humility to embrace the boundless potential within ourselves and one another.

Education, at its core, should not be a system of compliance, but an odyssey of discovery. When it sparks our imagination and stirs the depths of our hearts, learning transforms into something far greater than the mere acquisition of knowledge—it becomes a gateway to personal and collective evolution.

True education equips us with the tools to master the rhythms of daily life, granting us the wisdom to navigate both the seen and unseen complexities of the world. Yet beyond this pragmatic necessity, it holds within it the seeds of transformation—the power to unlock our latent potential, sharpen our talents, and guide us toward a life of depth, meaning, and purpose.

However, in our modern world, learning has become more of a burden than a joy. Instead of awakening curiosity, it often feels like a chore—an obligation imposed by institutions rather than an adventure undertaken by the mind and soul. We rarely pause to ask: Why do we seek to learn? What is the driving force behind our education? Is it the pursuit of knowledge for its own sake, or has it been reduced to a transactional endeavor—a means to an end rather than an experience of growth?

Education was never meant to be merely a preparation for survival. It was always meant to be the foundation upon which we build a life where we flourish, create, and contribute. But if that is true, why has learning become such a hassle?

Chapter 1

Why Learning is Such a Hassle!

"Education is the kindling of a flame, not the filling of a vessel."—**Socrates**

And yet, beyond the burdens of conventional education, deeper forms of learning whisper to us—elusive, luminous, beckoning us to transcend the rigid confines of the known and venture into the boundless expanse of possibility. This is the learning that does not merely fill the mind but awakens it, igniting the fire of curiosity and compelling us to push past the fragile perimeters of comfort. It is the kind of learning that sharpens intellect, fortifies reason, and grants us the rarest of gifts—the ability to sift truth from illusion, even in the midst of uncertainty.

But why, then, does learning so often feel like an uphill battle? Why do so many, after years spent within the halls of academia, emerge feeling estranged from knowledge itself? Why does something as elemental as curiosity—the very force that propels humanity forward—become a burden rather than a joy?

The truth is, learning is not a passive act; it is an act of defiance, of courage. To learn deeply is to step willingly into the unknown, to confront the discomfort of unlearning, to dismantle long-held beliefs and, in doing so, reconstruct the self. Yet, for many, education has been stripped of its transformative essence, reduced to a mechanical exercise—a rigid, formulaic system that constrains rather than liberates, conditions rather than awakens. It is no longer a process of self-expansion but a factory of conformity, where minds are molded into instruments of utility rather than cultivated as landscapes of boundless thought.

Learning should be an odyssey, a journey inward and outward—a voyage not only through the external world but through the hidden corridors of our own consciousness. It should be the art of becoming, an intimate act of self-discovery, a dance with wisdom, wonder, and the unknown.

Yet for far too many, it has become a burden, an obligation dictated by systems that measure intelligence in numbers and worth in credentials. It has become a series of tasks—a test to pass, a degree to obtain, a checklist to complete—its purpose obscured, its magic lost.

And so, we must ask ourselves: How did learning, the most natural of human pursuits, become so disconnected from the joy of discovery?

The System vs. the Soul of Learning

Education, as it exists today, is designed not for enlightenment, but for efficiency—a machine engineered to refine minds into cogs that fit neatly within the grand mechanisms of industry and economy. From the moment a child enters its gates, learning is framed not as a voyage of self-discovery, but as a transaction—a path to credentials, a stairway to employment, a measured ascent toward a predetermined future. It is not wisdom that is sought, but metrics: grades, diplomas, employability, social standing.

Yet a child, in their earliest years, is not bound by such constructs. They are born seekers, philosophers of their own unfolding world. They ask "why?" not as an obligation but as an instinct, their curiosity an unquenchable flame. They see the world with wonder, unfiltered and whole. But somewhere along the way, that raw, unrestrained hunger for knowledge is subdued, dulled, and systematically unlearned. The education system, in its cold precision, strips away the freedom of exploration and replaces it with obedience, memorization in place of imagination, standardization in place of originality.

And so, the great tragedy unfolds—not that we have failed to teach, but that we have taught too well the art of limitation.

Many mistake schooling for learning, but the two are not the same.

What We Are Told Education Is	What True Learning Should Be
A path to employment	A path to wisdom
A competition for grades	A journey of self-mastery
A system of memorization	A process of deep understanding
A pursuit of status	A pursuit of purpose
A means to an economic end	A lifelong quest for meaning

The modern system does not reward the mind that questions, only the mind that complies. Creativity is sacrificed at the altar of standardization, and originality is cast aside as inefficiency. The result? Graduates who have learned to pass tests but not to navigate life. They leave the institutions that shaped them armed with credentials yet burdened by uncertainty—educated in theory, but unprepared in essence. They have been taught what to think, but never how to think.

To reclaim the soul of education, we must return to the wisdom that predates the system—the wisdom that whispers from the pages of ancient texts, from the musings of poets, from the vast and intricate workings of nature itself. We must seek, not because we are told to, but because we are called to. For knowledge is not a ladder to be climbed; it is a fire to be lit, a river to be followed, a mystery to be unraveled.

And so, the path forward is clear: before we can truly learn, we must first remember how to wonder.

The Transformational Power of Learning

True learning, when infused with a selfless desire to serve, give, and love others, becomes transformative. It uplifts not just the mind, but also the soul. When learning is approached not with the intent of acquisition, but with the intent of expansion, something profound happens. The process no longer feels like a burden; it becomes a gateway to joy, inner peace, and a deep sense of purpose.

At its highest level, it is a form of alchemy—a transformation that does not merely add to our knowledge but changes who we are at our core. Science has even begun to recognize this in the form of epigenetics—the idea that our thoughts, behaviors, and experiences can literally alter the expression of our DNA, shaping not just our lives, but the lives of future generations. When we learn with the intent to grow, to evolve, to serve, we rewrite the very scripts of our existence.

This is the kind of learning that does not just add to the mind, but expands the soul. But to embrace this deeper form of learning, we must ask the essential question: Why do we seek knowledge at all?

The "Why" Behind Learning

At the heart of learning lies a question as ancient as time itself: why do we seek to know? What compels the human spirit to reach beyond the tangible, to unravel the unseen, to chase understanding as if it were the very air we breathe?

Is it survival, the primal instinct that drives us to acquire knowledge as a tool, a shield against uncertainty, a safeguard for the future? Is it ambition, that restless yearning to rise above, to carve our names into the fabric of history? Is it curiosity, the same unquenchable wonder that once filled our childhood days, when every shadow held a secret and every dawn whispered new mysteries? Is it fear, that silent force that propels us forward, pushing us to conquer ignorance before it renders us powerless? Or is it something deeper, something more luminous—the quiet, unwavering call to serve, to uplift, to weave our wisdom into the greater tapestry of humanity?

From the moment a child first peers into the world with wide, unburdened eyes, the why of learning is alive within them. They do not ask for wealth or titles. They do not seek knowledge for status or gain. They question because it is their nature, because the universe pulses with riddles, and they are compelled to answer. But somewhere along the way, this pure and fearless thirst for discovery is shackled by expectation. Knowledge is no longer a boundless horizon but a measure of worth, a stepping stone toward achievement, a means to an end. The fire that once burned wild is dimmed, subdued by the weight of systems that reward compliance over curiosity, memorization over understanding. What was once a journey of wonder becomes a race, where the finish line is not wisdom, but validation.

Yet, not all who seek knowledge do so with the same intent. Some learn to manipulate, to exploit, to bend the world to their will. Others learn to illuminate, to heal, to create. And so, the essence of learning is not found in knowledge itself, but in the spirit with which it is pursued. Information alone does not elevate the mind—it is the light within the seeker that transforms it into wisdom. Knowledge, when sought only for personal gain, remains hollow, a currency that buys influence but not depth, power but not purpose. If we seek learning only to serve the self, then we have merely expanded our intellect while allowing the soul to shrink.

But when we learn with the intent to give, to uplift, to contribute, something shifts. Knowledge ceases to be a possession and becomes a force. It ceases to be a burden and becomes a calling. Learning, then, is no longer an accumulation of facts, but a pilgrimage—a sacred unfolding that enriches not just the self, but the world. It becomes an offering, a bridge, a way to lift others as we rise. The mind expands not just in intellect, but in compassion. The heart learns as much as the brain.

Yet here lies the paradox. Even though we have built libraries that stretch beyond measure, what have we truly understood?

We have mapped the stars, but have we mapped our own hearts? We have unlocked the secrets of atoms, but have we unlocked the secrets of our own nature? We have chased progress to the edges of the earth, but in doing so, have we lost sight of what it means to be whole?

We live in an age of boundless knowledge, yet, are we truly wiser, happier, more fulfilled?

Our Apparent Accomplishments vs. The Reality of Our Accomplishments

Our Apparent Accomplishments	The Reality of Our Accomplishments
We gained vast amounts of knowledge	but still remain unconscious.
We earned billions	but never overcame our poverty mindset.
We lit zillions of lamps	but could not dispel the darkness within.
We passed thousands of laws	but never achieved justice.
We fell in love many times	but never became love itself.
We built millions of religious sanctuaries	but never understood spirituality.
We performed many good deeds	but never became goodness itself.
We celebrated many birthdays	but never truly lived a single moment.
We controlled vast empires	but never controlled our own destinies.
We conquered Everest and reached Mars	but never conquered ourselves.
We created powerful defense forces	but never achieved peace.

Our Apparent Accomplishments	The Reality of Our Accomplishments
We earned Masters and PhDs	but remain ignorant about ourselves.
We made technological breakthroughs	but could never decipher our own lives.

Some might argue, "This doesn't apply to me!" Yet the truth is, it applies to us all. Why? Because none of us have fully uncovered the essence of who we truly are. The veils of illusion still obscure our understanding, leaving us disconnected from the clarity and depth that lies within.

Learning as a Path to Wisdom

The journey of learning is not merely the acquisition of knowledge or the attainment of external success—it is a pilgrimage inward, a search for the hidden truths that shape the very essence of our existence. It is the slow, deliberate unfolding of the self, a revelation that reaches beyond facts and figures into the depths of who we are and who we are yet to become.

To truly transform ourselves and, by extension, the world around us, we must venture beyond the surface of education and into its soul. It is not enough to ask what we learn—we must ask how we learn, why we learn, and what unseen forces shape the architecture of our minds. For within this silent, often unconscious shaping lies the blueprint of our potential and the boundaries of our limitations. Only by understanding this hidden framework can we break free from the constraints of conditioned thought and step into a fuller, more profound way of being.

Learning must no longer be seen as a mere transaction, a means to an end, a stepping stone to security or status. It must be redefined as a lifelong odyssey—one that intertwines the external pursuit of knowledge with the internal quest for wisdom. It must be a practice of both expansion and introspection, a dance between discovery and self-mastery. For only when knowledge is infused with meaning does it cease to be a burden and become a guiding light.

If we dare to walk this path, we may finally learn not just how to exist, but how to truly live. And perhaps, just perhaps, we will awaken the courage to embrace our dual roles as both students and teachers in the ever-unfolding story of life, illuminating not only our own way forward but also the paths of generations yet to come.

This brings us to an essential question: How does learning shape not just what we know, but who we are? Does it merely sharpen our intellect, or does it sculpt the very essence of our being? Does it leave fleeting traces of knowledge, or does it carve deep imprints upon our character, our values, our sense of self?

For learning is not merely an external pursuit—it is an inner metamorphosis, a transformation both subtle and profound, shaping us in ways both seen and unseen, molding the spirit as much as the mind, refining the soul as much as the intellect. It is the great unseen force that not only changes how we think but who we become.

Chapter 2

The Formation of Our Core Character

The arc of life and the arc of education are deeply intertwined, each shaping the other in subtle, profound ways. Learning never truly ceases; it is an eternal current, flowing through the corridors of time, molding our thoughts, refining our perspectives, and weaving itself into the very fabric of who we are. Life, in its infinite complexity, is both the teacher and the lesson, offering us unending opportunities for growth. Schools play a vital role in this process, yet education is more than a collection of facts, more than a staircase leading to career success, more than an instrument for material achievement. It is the unseen force that sculpts character, the compass that orients us toward meaning, the foundation upon which we build the essence of our existence. Nations across the world take pride in their education systems, believing they offer the finest intellectual training to their citizens. But is education merely the transfer of knowledge, or does it hold a far greater power—one that extends beyond intellect and into the formation of identity itself?

Education is not simply the memorization of information; it is the lens through which we perceive reality, the space where imagination, creativity, intuition, and critical thought converge. Throughout our educational journey, we are meant to:

Discover our unique identity—the distinctiveness that sets us apart in an ocean of humanity.

Develop a strong core character—the foundation upon which all decisions, actions, and values rest.

Unveil our true self—the essence buried beneath layers of conditioning and expectation.

Grasp our intrinsic, unshakable values—the moral compass that guides us even when the path is uncertain.

9

Recognize our innate talents—the gifts we were meant to nurture, refine, and share.

Root ourselves in life's deeper purpose—not in the pursuit of fleeting possessions, accolades, or fame, but in something greater than ourselves.

Expand our perception beyond what is visible—to learn to see the invisible, hear the unheard, and understand the unknowable.

But is this what truly happens? Or are we, instead, shaped by an education system that conditions us to follow prescribed formulas, equipping us with tools but not with wisdom, teaching us to conform but not to question? Does this system, like an unseen hand, shape the personas we adopt, the choices we make, the character we embody?

Before we examine the education system itself, we must first consider a mystery that has perplexed scientists, philosophers, and parents alike: why do two individuals—raised in the same environment, exposed to the same teachings—develop into entirely different people, walking divergent paths, driven by opposing values?

A Story of Divergent Paths

Lisa and James were the proud parents of twin boys, Brian and Peter. From the moment they were born, people marveled at the twins' bright eyes and boundless curiosity. Their hands eagerly reached out to explore the world, their faces lighting up at the sound of new voices. Always moving in perfect harmony, Brian and Peter were inseparable.

As they grew, so did their bond. They were like two stars orbiting each other, inseparable in their pursuits, mirroring one another's steps. Their thirst for knowledge was unmatched. While other children's attention flitted from one distraction to another, Brian and Peter immersed themselves in whatever captured their fascination, their world consisting mainly of each other.

Lisa and James, elated by their sons' potential, dreamed of greatness for them—Nobel Prizes, monumental discoveries, world-changing achievements. But despite their shared brilliance, something peculiar began to unfold: their personalities, once indistinguishable, began to diverge.

Peter was bold, fearless, and determined, always eager to conquer challenges without hesitation. Brian, in contrast, was cautious, his brow furrowing with concern at the unknown. He preferred to observe from the sidelines before stepping forward, relying on Peter's lead.

As time passed, these differences solidified. Peter became confident and assertive, while Brian grew increasingly hesitant, tethered to his brother's courage yet unable to claim his own. Their closeness remained, but their paths had already begun to separate.

When the boys turned three, they were enrolled in an advanced daycare, situated on the grounds of a golf resort just a block from their home. The daycare catered to children with exceptional abilities, offering a rich curriculum and a vast outdoor play area. It was here, on an ordinary afternoon, that an extraordinary event occurred— one that would carve an indelible mark upon their identities.

While playing outside, a large German Shepherd escaped from the resort's dog area and charged toward the children. Panic erupted. Teachers rushed to gather the terrified children inside while resort staff sprinted after the dog, desperately trying to catch it. Brian and Peter, sitting together on the grass, watched in frozen terror as the animal locked eyes with them and sprinted toward them, teeth bared, barking ferociously.

Brian's body turned to stone, fear paralyzing him where he sat. His mind screamed for him to run, but his legs refused to obey. Peter, sensing the imminent danger, grabbed Brian's arm, urging him to move. But when Brian remained rooted in place, Peter did the only thing he could—he stepped between his brother and the charging beast, standing tall, his small frame radiating defiance. He clenched his fists and barked back at the dog with all the force his tiny voice could muster.

The dog hesitated, confused by this sudden display of resistance. It was just enough time for the staff to reach them and restrain the animal.

The incident left a scar on their spirits, an unseen but undeniable imprint. Brian, already cautious, withdrew further, retreating into his own fears. Peter, on the other hand, found in himself a newfound strength—an unshakable belief in his ability to protect, to take charge, to act. In that moment, without realizing it, the trajectory of their lives had been set.

The Science of Character Formation

Years passed, and the twins, now young men, embarked on their academic journeys. Both were accepted into Ivy League universities, their brilliance earning them prestigious scholarships. Peter pursued medicine, specializing in genetics and pediatrics, eager to change lives. Brian, drawn to technology, immersed himself in artificial intelligence and cryptocurrency, fascinated by the possibilities of the digital world.

Despite walking through the same university halls, their lives followed opposing currents. Peter thrived, immersing himself in humanitarian projects, traveling to underdeveloped nations, using his knowledge to serve those in need. Brian, meanwhile, grew increasingly isolated, retreating from the world of human connection into the limitless realm of algorithms and blockchain networks. His genius made him highly sought after, yet his detachment deepened.

And then, the inevitable reckoning arrived.

Brian, once the child paralyzed by fear, now sought control—not over himself, but over systems, over wealth, over the intangible flow of digital power. He orchestrated a scheme so intricate that financial institutions failed to detect it for years. When his empire of deception finally crumbled, it did so spectacularly.

News headlines screamed his name. Cameras flashed as officers stormed his apartment, seizing hard drives, laptops, stacks of untraceable cash. The world watched as he was led away in handcuffs, his head bowed under the weight of his choices.

Peter, heartbroken, returned home to console his parents. Lisa and James stood in disbelief, struggling to reconcile the image of the brilliant, curious child they had raised with the man now imprisoned behind cold steel bars.

The Role of Epigenetics in Shaping Character

Their confusion mirrors the experiences of many parents, teachers, and researchers. How can children raised under identical conditions—nurtured under the same roof, taught the same lessons, and given the same opportunities—grow into individuals with vastly different values, personalities, and life paths? This paradox has puzzled minds across disciplines, from psychology to genetics, from philosophy to neuroscience.

Traditional explanations point to an intricate web of factors—parenting style, family dynamics, life events, social influences, and even the unpredictable nature of free will. But as we delve deeper, we find that there is something far more fundamental at work, something unseen yet omnipresent—an invisible but powerful force shaping the architecture of who we become.

This force is encoded within us, yet it is not fixed. It is a fluid, ever-changing interplay between nature and nurture, between inheritance and experience, between the predetermined and the malleable. It is here that science introduces us to one of its most profound revelations: epigenetics—the study of how our environment, experiences, and choices do not just influence us psychologically, but biologically, altering the very expression of our genes.

How Experience Rewrites Our Genetic Code

For centuries, the prevailing belief was that genetics alone determined our destiny—a rigid script written at birth, immutable and absolute. But modern research has rewritten this notion. Scientists now understand that while our DNA provides the foundational blueprint, it is not an unalterable fate.

Every moment of our existence leaves an imprint not just on our minds but on our very biology. As we grow, our DNA accumulates chemical marks—a molecular language that tells our genes when to activate, how much to express, and when to remain silent. These marks form what is known as the epigenome, a dynamic system that responds to everything we experience—love, stress, trauma, education, relationships, nourishment, and even the thoughts we dwell upon.

It is the reason why identical twins, who share the same genetic blueprint, can develop entirely different behaviors, health outcomes, and life trajectories. One may become an optimist, resilient in the face of hardship, while the other may struggle with depression. One may excel in leadership, driven by confidence and ambition, while the other retreats into solitude, burdened by self-doubt. The difference lies not in their genes but in the way their life experiences rearrange the epigenetic markers that determine how those genes are expressed.

The Early Years: A Crucial Window of Development

If genes are the notes on a musical score, then epigenetics is the conductor that determines how the melody of life is played. And just as a symphony is shaped by its earliest movements, the human psyche is molded most profoundly in childhood.

Researchers have found that young children's brains are especially sensitive to epigenetic changes during the critical early years of rapid development. The neural pathways that shape cognition, emotional intelligence, and social behavior are formed long before a child even understands the world they are stepping into.

Carl Jung, the great Swiss psychoanalyst, emphasized that the first seven years of a child's life are crucial for the development of the unconscious mind—a realm where deeply ingrained beliefs, values, and behavioral patterns take root. This aligns with Sigmund Freud's theories, which suggest that unresolved conflicts or traumas from these formative years can shape a child's unconscious drives and fears, manifesting in their relationships, ambitions, and emotional well-being throughout life.

Modern neuroscience has confirmed what these early psychological pioneers intuited: childhood experiences do not just shape memory and perception; they sculpt the biological framework of the brain itself. They influence whether a child will grow into an adult who approaches life with confidence or hesitation, with resilience or fragility, with empathy or detachment.

A nurturing and loving environment enhances the expression of genes linked to emotional stability, intelligence, and overall well-being. Meanwhile, chronic stress, neglect, or fear can trigger the suppression or activation of genetic pathways associated with anxiety, depression, or aggression. It is a sobering realization—one that places immense responsibility on those who guide children through their earliest years.

At our most fundamental biological level, it becomes undeniably clear: environment is not just a backdrop—it is a sculptor of identity. And yet, a deeper question remains: how do we create educational spaces that awaken not just knowledge, but wisdom, resilience, and compassion in every child?

To answer this, we must journey inward—into the silent codes that govern our biology, the ancestral rhythms of fear and love, the ancient dance between survival and surrender. For it is there, in the unseen chambers of human nature, that the true architecture of education is laid—not in classrooms, but in consciousness.

Chapter 3

It's More than Just Biology

At its core, life is an unceasing dance of survival—a delicate interplay between existence and extinction, between continuity and dissolution. Whether at the level of the individual, the society, the species, or the intricate web of life that binds our planetary system, all things move to the rhythm of preservation and endurance. Beneath the surface of human behavior, this relentless pursuit of security manifests in myriad ways, shaping our thoughts, our actions, and the very fabric of our identities.

The first and most primal of these insecurities is rooted in the fear of physical survival—a deep, subconscious awareness of life's inevitable transience, a whisper of mortality that lingers in the backdrop of every human endeavor. The body, fragile and finite, reminds us that time is an unforgiving force, and so we strive—sometimes desperately—to fortify ourselves against its inexorable pull.

The second insecurity, subtler yet no less formidable, is the fear of fading into silence—the quiet dissolution of the carefully constructed self-image, the loss of personal significance, the vanishing of the identity we have so painstakingly curated. We fear not merely the cessation of life, but the end of meaning—the unraveling of the story we have wrapped around our name.

And so, much of humanity remains ensnared in a relentless defense of identity, mistaking it for self-esteem, illusion for essence. In this unconscious struggle, we shape a world where security is measured in countless forms—wealth, status, power, relationships—each of us building fortresses of certainty around our fears. Yet these fortresses are fragile, built upon the shifting sands of perception, molded by the echoes of past experiences and the inherited narratives of those who raised us.

The Early Roots of Insecurity

From the moment we take our first breath, we begin constructing our understanding of safety and danger, of belonging and rejection. The earliest imprints of fear—whether through harsh words, loud noises, neglect, or a sense of abandonment—take root in the depths of our subconscious, shaping the lens through which we view the world. These impressions, whether large or small, etch themselves into the architecture of our developing minds, forming the foundation of our insecurities.

In today's hyper-connected, overstimulated world, the environment in which a child is raised—its emotional climate, the stability of relationships, the unspoken tensions and expectations—plays a profound role in determining their sense of security. Modern parenting, often shaped by societal pressures and the digital age, unintentionally deepens these insecurities. In a May 2024 article for MSN News, Samantha Jenkins identified key parenting trends that contribute to emotional fragility in children:

- Doing everything for them
- Overprotecting them
- Failing to set boundaries
- Spoiling them
- Avoiding difficult conversations
- Micromanaging their lives
- Ignoring emotional intelligence
- Diminishing their feelings
- Overemphasizing achievement

Children raised in such environments often struggle to navigate adversity, lacking the resilience to withstand the inevitable trials of life. Many seek refuge in distraction—social media, video games, fleeting pleasures—avoiding discomfort rather than confronting it. As a result, the world becomes a place to fear rather than explore, a landscape of obstacles rather than opportunities.

The Constructed Self and the Quest for Survival

The drive for survival is not merely biological—it is deeply psychological, sculpted by the narratives of self-worth and identity instilled in us by family, culture, and education. From childhood, we are taught to compete, to prove ourselves, to establish an identity that is valuable in the eyes of others. Rarely are we told that we are already whole, that we are already enough, that our worth is not contingent upon external validation.

Paradoxically, the more tightly we cling to the constructed self, the more fragile it becomes. We live in fear of irrelevance, of being overshadowed, of becoming ordinary. Consider the celebrated rock star, standing atop the world, basking in fame, wealth, and adoration—yet beneath the glittering facade, tormented by a haunting question: Will I still matter tomorrow? They do not fear failure so much as they fear disappearance. The death they dread is not physical—it is the fading of their significance, the dissolution of the persona they have become.

But this existential fear is not unique to celebrities. It is woven into the human condition. The executive fears losing power. The scholar fears being forgotten. The artist fears becoming obsolete. We grasp at permanence in an impermanent world, blind to the truth that the very self we are trying to preserve is a construct—an illusion we mistake for reality.

From childhood, we are conditioned to derive meaning through comparison. Success is framed as standing taller than others, earning admiration, accumulating achievements. But the irony of the false self is that the more it seeks to be fed, the more insatiable it becomes. The pursuit of validation turns into a hunger that is never satisfied, leaving us in a cycle of striving, achieving, fearing, and defending.

The Balance Between Security and Survival

Most of us do not consciously dwell on the fear of death or the fragility of self-worth, but these anxieties hum quietly beneath the surface, influencing every decision. We mask them beneath the routines of daily life—paying bills, maintaining careers, sustaining relationships—yet a quiet urgency lingers beneath it all.

From birth, our first cries are not just for oxygen, but for nourishment, connection, safety. If these needs are not met, the void they leave is not merely physical but emotional. Over time, these voids harden into insecurities, shaping how we engage with the world. Some of us react by retreating into isolation, others by overcompensating—seeking control, dominance, or recognition to shield against hidden fears.

Much of the conflict we see in the world today—whether in politics, business, or personal relationships—is not born of malice but of competing insecurities. The deeper our fears, the more we seek to protect ourselves. But protection often comes in the form of control, aggression, and self-deception, distorting our perception of reality and deepening our suffering.

The Roots of Character

The story of Peter and Brian serves as a stark illustration of these dynamics. Raised in the same environment, one brother found his security in service, the other in self-preservation. Peter's choices stemmed from a deep inner confidence, an alignment between his actions and his authentic self. Brian, consumed by fear, sought security in deception, convinced that power and control could insulate him from his insecurities. But in the end, his actions did not free him—they only magnified his fear, leading to consequences that reinforced his inner turmoil.

Their story illuminates a universal truth: our environments shape us, but we are not prisoners of them. Even within the same upbringing, individuals form radically different perceptions, values, and habits. By the age of seven, our core character is largely formed— not just by what is taught, but by what is absorbed through subtle emotional exchanges, unspoken tensions, and the atmospheres in which we are raised. These early years etch deep grooves into the subconscious, shaping how we interpret and engage with the world.

At its essence, character is shaped by two forces:

1. **Inherent Uniqueness** – The innate qualities we are born with, shaping how we perceive and respond to the world.
2. **Learned Behavior** – The "software" programmed into us through cultural conditioning—often rooted in fear, expectation, and societal structures.

Traditional education, however, focuses almost entirely on intellectual mastery, while neglecting the inner architecture of the soul. It teaches children what to achieve, but not who they are at their core. It offers the instruments of success but withholds the mirror of self-discovery.

But if we are not merely our bodies, our achievements, or our carefully curated identities, then who are we?

This question, like a quiet whisper beneath the noise of daily existence, calls us to go beyond what we know, beyond insecurity, beyond survival itself. It invites us to confront the illusions and unconscious habits that govern our lives and to awaken to the truth that has always been quietly waiting beneath them.

And so, as we move forward, we must ask ourselves: Are we the architects of our destiny—or the unconscious inheritors of patterns we never chose? The journey ahead will unravel this question, inviting us to reclaim the deeper truths hidden within our habitual conditioning—and, perhaps, to rediscover the self we were always meant to become.

Chapter 4

Living Our Knowledge vs. Living Our Habits

Childhood, that fleeting and fragile dawn of life, unfolds in stages, each one shaping the mind and spirit in ways both subtle and profound. It is during these formative years that we begin to lay the foundations of our cognitive abilities, learning to navigate the world, solve problems, and forge the social and emotional connections that will guide us through life. Every encounter, every triumph, and every wound leaves its mark, silently crafting the architecture of our emerging worldview.

But beneath the surface of this learning, something even more powerful is at work—something deeper than the facts we absorb or the skills we develop. Within the first seven years of life, the subconscious mind is at its most impressionable, acting as an open field in which the seeds of lifelong behavior, perception, and identity are sown. These years serve as the silent scripting of our internal "software," shaping how we will engage with the world long before we gain the awareness to question it.

It is not only the lessons spoken to a child that shape them, but the unspoken ones—the glances exchanged, the emotions suppressed, the fears carried, the love given or withheld. Children do not merely listen; they observe, absorb, and internalize. They inherit not only their parents' words, but their habits, their reactions, and their unspoken beliefs about life. And so, the foundation is laid—sometimes consciously, but more often as an invisible force, guiding their choices, their fears, and ultimately, the lives they build.

Some traits remain fluid, evolving with time and experience, while others solidify, hardening into patterns so deeply embedded that they become mistaken for identity itself. These patterns, forged in the fires of early experience, shape our reality—not through what we know, but through the habits we unconsciously adopt.

True Fact: We Don't Live Our Knowledge—We Live Our Habits

Consider this truth: we do not live according to the knowledge we acquire, but rather, we live according to the habits we form. Knowledge may illuminate the path before us, but it is habit that dictates the direction we take.

A person may know the value of patience, yet habitually react with frustration. They may understand the importance of honesty, yet find themselves falling into deception. They may recognize the necessity of exercise, yet still remain sedentary. The disconnect between knowledge and action is one of the greatest paradoxes of human nature: we are not what we know; we are what we repeatedly do.

Habits, once ingrained, become the unseen architects of our lives. They free the brain from the burden of constant decision-making, allowing us to move through the world on autopilot. This efficiency is a double-edged sword—while some habits support growth, others create invisible walls that confine us, limiting our potential and reinforcing cycles that no longer serve us.

Yet, most people rarely question the routines that govern their lives. They wake up each day and follow the same patterns, not because they consciously choose to, but because these behaviors have been etched into their neural pathways, repeated so often that they have become second nature. These habits do not simply shape how we live—they shape who we become. Addictions, for example, are a clear case of repeated behaviors that spiral out of control, trapping individuals in cycles that are hard to break.

The beliefs we inherit from society, family, and culture act as unseen sculptors, molding our perceptions, instincts, and automatic responses. These inherited patterns often provide an emotional cushion, an illusion of stability in an ever-changing world. Some habits soothe us, wrapping us in the familiar warmth of routine, while others tighten like a noose, binding us to patterns that erode our well-being. Yet, regardless of whether they empower us or imprison us, these behaviors are not immutable. They can be examined, dismantled, and reshaped—if we have the courage to unravel the emotional threads that bind them to our sense of self.

While habits offer comfort, they also test the boundaries of our evolution. To rely too heavily upon them is to risk becoming stagnant, lulled into a state of unconscious repetition. Even the most enlightened minds can be ensnared by destructive behaviors, not due to a lack of understanding, but because ingrained routines overpower conscious will. Knowledge alone cannot rescue us—it must be lived, embodied, and woven into the fabric of our daily existence. Only then does wisdom cease to be a concept and become the force that propels us toward true transformation.

The Stark Truth About Habits and Fear

Mahatma Gandhi once observed:

> "Watch your thoughts, for they become your words.
> Watch your words, for they become your actions.
> Watch your actions, for they become your habits.
> Watch your habits, for they become your character.
> Watch your character, for it becomes your destiny."

At the core of many habits lies an unspoken force: fear. Fear of failure, of loss, of insignificance. Fear of stepping outside the familiar, of confronting the unknown, of becoming vulnerable. This fear, buried deep within our subconscious, dictates our responses, our decisions, and ultimately, the course of our lives.

In our attempt to shield ourselves from discomfort, we turn to habit as a refuge, a predictable rhythm in an unpredictable world. We seek security through repetition, mistaking the familiar for the safe. Yet in doing so, we often surrender our growth, allowing fear to weave itself into the fabric of our identity.

The pursuit of security often morphs into the pursuit of superiority—whether through wealth, power, or recognition. The constructed self, ever fragile, demands external validation, leading us into endless competition for status. This struggle for significance manifests in every sphere—religion, politics, business, relationships—each one a battleground for the insecure self to assert its worth. But true security cannot be found in dominance, nor in avoidance. It is not won through control, nor through withdrawal. It is only found in liberation—from fear, from false narratives, from the illusions we mistake for truth.

Thriving Beyond Survival

To exist is one thing—to thrive is another. The pursuit of knowledge must be paired with the courage to change, for wisdom lies not in what we accumulate, but in what we apply. And if we are to apply what we know, we must first recognize the universal law that governs all things: the law of change.

Everything in existence is in motion, shifting and evolving with each passing moment. The cells in our bodies, the landscapes of the earth, the constellations above—all are in a perpetual state of transformation. And yet, as human beings, we resist change. We cling to what is known, fearing what is yet to come. But change is not the enemy—it is the catalyst for growth, the gateway to possibility.

To thrive is to embrace this inevitability. It is to recognize that we are not bound by our past, nor by the habits that have shaped us thus far. Every moment offers a choice—to remain as we are, or to step beyond the confines of familiarity into the realm of transformation.

Living intentionally means becoming conscious of the habits that no longer serve us. It means questioning the patterns we have inherited, breaking free from the inertia of routine, and choosing to cultivate habits that align with our deepest truths. For true freedom does not lie in knowing—it lies in becoming.

Change is the birthplace of transformation—the silent doorway through which progress whispers its arrival. It beckons us beyond the familiar cadence of routine, inviting us to step into the vast unknown, where potential is boundless and growth becomes inevitable. In the arms of change, we are no longer prisoners of habit, but architects of a more conscious destiny.

And so, this journey of awakening now leads us to a deeper exploration—not just of change as a concept, but of its sacred function in the evolution of learning and life itself. If habit dictates the rhythm of our days, then change is the song that sets us free—the force that dissolves stagnation, reshapes our reality, and unlocks the infinite capacity to learn, grow, and live with intention.

Chapter 5

The Power of Change

To confront the power of change, we must embrace a lifelong commitment to learning. We are not mere passengers on this journey; we are eternal students, bound to curiosity like the stars are bound to the night. It is curiosity that propels us toward the unknown, guiding us beyond the borders of certainty and into the infinite landscape of possibility. Each day, whether marked by grand revelations or quiet whispers of insight, unfolds with a lesson. Like the ever-expanding universe, our understanding stretches outward, reminding us that the limits we perceive are merely thresholds waiting to be crossed.

But true learning—the kind that transforms both self and society—must be conscious, purposeful, and imbued with a deeper mission. Without this, knowledge remains fragmented, a mere collection of facts without coherence, like scattered stars without constellations. Half-knowledge, untethered from wisdom, becomes a dangerous thing, masquerading as power while lacking the foundation of understanding. It is in this incomplete grasp of truth that we risk not building but undoing, drilling holes where foundations should be laid.

The Consequence of Incomplete Understanding

Let me share a story that echoes this truth.

Years ago, as part of a cultural exchange program, I hosted a guest from a remote region—a man unacquainted with the technological conveniences we take for granted. The program was designed to expose individuals to modern tools and ideas so they could return to their communities with knowledge that could uplift and empower.

One day, my guest watched me repair a broken pipe using a cordless drill. His eyes lit up at the sight of this seemingly magical device. He listened intently as I explained how it worked, nodding with enthusiasm.

Moments later, duty called me away, and when I returned, I found my worktable riddled with holes—dozens of them. In his excitement, my guest had taken the drill and, without understanding its purpose, had wielded it as a force of sheer action rather than thoughtful creation.

Education, like my drill, is a tool. Yet, without purpose and understanding, it is wielded blindly, leading to destruction rather than transformation. Too often, society resembles that table—riddled with holes, punctured by the misguided use of knowledge, where understanding was meant to be the thread that holds us together. Instead of addressing these voids, we cover them with distractions and temporary fixes. But a patched surface does not heal what lies beneath; it merely delays the inevitable reckoning.

What if, instead of concealing these holes, we mended them with the threads of true education—education that does not merely inform but reawakens? What if we did not seek to simply fill minds but to illuminate them, weaving a tapestry of wisdom rather than a scattered landscape of facts?

To begin such a reawakening, we must first attune ourselves to the universe's unbending laws—principles that govern not only stars and seasons, but the rhythms of growth, learning, and life itself. Only then can we align education with these timeless truths and restore its power to transform, uplift, and unite.

The Role of Education in Transformation

Our current education system claims to guide us through this grand exploration, to be the bridge between ignorance and understanding. It is meant to be a playground of discovery, a laboratory for the mind, a sacred space where curiosity is cultivated, and the unseen dimensions of thought are revealed. Yet, is this truly happening? Or have we built a system that, instead of nurturing wonder, entombs it beneath layers of procedure, rote memorization, and sterile assessments?

For twelve or more years, we tell our students that education will prepare them for life. That at the end of this structured journey, they will emerge ready—ready to build careers, contribute to society, and find meaning. Yet, the world tells a different story. What we see is a landscape of disconnection, a world brimming with knowledge but starved of wisdom. A society abundant in information yet impoverished in empathy.

Our habits, both conscious and unconscious, are the products of our experiences, environments, and the insecurities we nurture. We develop routines, seeking comfort in their repetition, even as we long for the unknown. This paradox of desiring both stability and adventure is reflected in our education system. Students, caught in this tension, oscillate between engagement and apathy, craving meaning but often finding none.

The subjects we deem essential—history, mathematics, science, and civics—are often reduced to mechanical exercises, stripped of their deeper purpose. Instead of revealing the interconnected beauty of existence, they are fragmented into lifeless tasks, obstacles to be endured rather than mysteries to be explored.

Consider a child learning about ecosystems. Instead of being immersed in nature, feeling the pulse of life in the soil beneath their fingertips, they are handed definitions to memorize. The symphony of interdependence, the sacred rhythm of life itself, is flattened into mere terminology. Similarly, history is often reduced to a collection of dates and battles, missing the heartbeat of human triumphs and failures, the ebb and flow of civilizations that mirror our own struggles and aspirations.

Redefining the Path Forward

But there is another way. A path that does not confine us to the limits of what is already known, but instead dares us to step beyond them.

This path is one of continual expansion—of seeking, questioning, and adding value with every thought and action. It is a path where learning is not a means to an end but the very fabric of existence itself.

To rebuild education, we must step beyond the rigid walls of tradition. We must cultivate a system that does not merely prepare students for a profession but prepares them for life—to think, to feel, to connect. A complete education does not just impart knowledge; it awakens wisdom. It aligns with the fundamental laws of the universe, guiding us toward a higher purpose—one rooted not in ambition alone, but in self-discovery and the service of something greater than ourselves.

Imagine a world where students learn by doing—where they cultivate gardens to understand biology, debate ethical dilemmas to explore philosophy, and build communities rather than compete for superficial achievements. Imagine an education system that teaches not just how to solve problems, but how to approach life with courage, empathy, and creativity.

If insecurity forms the foundation of our education, then all we produce are tools misused, wielded in service of the false self and fear. But if we build an education system on the bedrock of self-awareness and purpose, the tools we gain will be used not to create chaos but to craft beauty—to uplift, to serve, to illuminate. We will become the architects of a more compassionate world, empowering others to step into their own potential and weave their own part of the grand tapestry of life.

One example of this transformation comes from a school that replaced traditional grading with a portfolio system. Instead of chasing scores, students documented their learning through projects, reflections, and self-assessments. The results were profound: students not only retained more information but engaged with their studies with newfound passion and purpose.

Another story speaks of a program that introduced mindfulness into classrooms. Initially met with skepticism, it soon revealed its power—reducing stress, improving focus, and strengthening relationships. Students began to see education not as a burden, but as a journey inward as well as outward. They realized that true learning is not just about the mind; it is about the heart.

Ultimately, education is not about filling empty spaces—it is about weaving meaning into the very fabric of our existence. It is about recognizing that our truest calling is not merely to accumulate knowledge, but to understand ourselves and our place within the grand symphony of life. When we view education as an ever-unfolding journey—one fueled by curiosity and anchored in purpose—we align ourselves with the infinite potential of change. A power as vast, as transformative, and as boundless as the universe itself.

Chapter 6

Who or What Guides Our Education System?

Our education system leads us down a familiar, well-trodden path—a journey meticulously designed to acquaint us with the knowledge of the world. It presents itself as a map, a carefully drawn blueprint of human understanding, offering glimpses into the wonders of nature, the marvels of science, and the labyrinthine corridors of history. And yet, for all its breadth, this system often lingers at the surface, a vast but shallow sea, sparkling with information but rarely inviting us to dive into its depths.

What lies beyond this structured curriculum? What hidden dimensions remain unseen, awaiting those who dare to look deeper?

We navigate the ocean of knowledge much like ships gliding effortlessly across its glittering expanse. We marvel at the ripples, the transient reflections, the surface currents that guide us forward, yet we seldom plunge beneath the waves to explore the intricate ecosystems teeming below. Beneath this shimmering façade lies a world of interconnectedness, a realm of depth and mystery that reveals its secrets only to those courageous enough to surrender to its currents.

This kind of immersion—the kind that allows us to feel the pulse of knowledge rather than simply memorize its abstractions—often begins in higher education. It is here, in the pursuit of specialization, that the doors to deeper understanding seem to open. Yet even within these institutions, we are funneled into narrow streams of expertise, like divers descending into a single trench, losing sight of the vast, interconnected ocean that surrounds us.

The Fragmentation of Knowledge

This relentless focus on specialization, while undeniably valuable, comes at a cost. It produces experts in isolated domains but leaves them disconnected from the broader web of wisdom that binds everything together. A marine biologist may devote their life to studying a single species, an oceanographer may chart the restless movements of currents, and a geologist may map the seabed—but rarely do they come together to perceive the ocean as a single, living entity.

This pattern extends beyond the natural sciences into all disciplines. Economists analyze human behavior through financial models, philosophers explore the nature of existence, artists seek to express universal truths through their craft—yet these inquiries often remain in isolation, missing the profound revelations that arise when knowledge converges.

Life's deepest truths do not reside within the walls of any single discipline; they emerge at the intersections, where seemingly disparate fields merge, where ideas flow into one another like tributaries into a great river. It is in these moments of convergence that we truly begin to understand the world—not as a collection of fragmented subjects, but as a grand, interwoven masterpiece.

Yet, despite this reality, our education system remains fixated on compartmentalization. Students are funneled into rigid categories, encouraged to master specific skills at the expense of holistic understanding. The system rewards specialization over synthesis, expertise over exploration. In doing so, it fosters a worldview that sees life in isolated parts rather than as an interconnected whole.

If we are to truly embrace the depths of learning, we must abandon this artificial separation and move toward a more integrated, fluid approach to education. Just as the natural world thrives through delicate interdependencies, so too must human knowledge evolve—not as a collection of isolated fields but as a unified pursuit of truth.

The Student Experience: Endurance or Exploration?

At the heart of this issue lies the experience of students themselves. For many, school is not a sanctuary of discovery, nor a garden where curiosity is nurtured, but a waiting room—something to be endured until life begins. The subjects offered—history, mathematics, science, literature—often feel disconnected from reality, perceived as obstacles to overcome rather than gateways to wonder.

This disconnection is not imagined; research confirms it. According to the Yale Center for Emotional Intelligence, nearly 75% of students report negative feelings about school, with words like stressed, tired, and bored dominating their descriptions. Another survey reveals that many students view their classes as either irrelevant or too abstract, highlighting a chasm between the knowledge they acquire and the life they are expected to navigate.

And so, rather than igniting a hunger for understanding, education often extinguishes it. Instead of cultivating critical thinking, creativity, and self-inquiry, it produces graduates who feel unprepared for the complexities of existence. The flame of curiosity—the light that should guide them on their lifelong journey—is dimmed before it has a chance to burn brightly.

The Two Paths of Education

When we ask, "Who or what guides our education system?" the answer is twofold:

1. The First Path leads to a fragmented, pseudo-reality governed by the "What's in it for me?" mindset. This is the path of self-interest, short-term goals, and shallow understanding. It prioritizes specialization over synthesis, competition over collaboration, and individual success over collective wisdom. It is a path that deepens the illusion of separation, leaving us disconnected from the deeper truths of existence.
2. The Second Path beckons us into a realm of wholeness, where knowledge is not confined to isolated disciplines

but woven into the intricate tapestry of existence. It calls us to rise beyond the narrow corridors of specialization and embrace the symphony of interconnected wisdom, guided by the question: "What am I here to give?" This path does not measure success by mere memorization or mastery; instead, it seeks to infuse learning with purpose, transforming it from an accumulation of facts into a lifelong unfolding of insight. It urges us not only to comprehend the world but to move in harmony with its rhythms—to see learning not as a destination, but as a living, breathing journey toward wisdom, one that deepens with every step we take.

The path we choose—whether we remain on the surface, driven by self-interest, or plunge into the deeper currents of universal wisdom—will shape not only our individual lives but the destiny of humanity itself. If we choose wisely, education can become something far greater than a tool for specialization; it can become a force of connection, meaning, and transformation.

The Illusion of Separation

Our five senses, though powerful, offer only a fragmented view of reality. They show us what is near, what is tangible, what fits within the narrow frame of our immediate perception. But they do not reveal the vast web that binds all things together.

And yet, we move through life as though we are separate—isolated beings adrift in a world of competition, striving for resources, validation, and control. We erect artificial barriers—between disciplines, between nations, between hearts—mistaking division for strength. We measure success not by the depth of our contribution to the whole, but by how high we climb above others, blind to the truth that our ascent means little if it is not in service of something greater than ourselves.

This is the great illusion of our age—the belief that we are alone. That our actions exist in isolation. That we are distinct from the universe that bore us. But beneath this illusion lies an undeniable truth: we are part of something vast, something ancient, something interconnected. The very atoms that form our bodies were forged in the hearts of long-dead stars. The air we breathe was once inhaled by those who came before us. The rivers that flow today are the same that nourished the first civilizations. Life, at its core, is not about separation, but about unity.

The Call for Transformation

If we are to transcend the illusion of separation, our approach to education must undergo not just reform, but a renaissance—an awakening that shifts its very foundation from division to unity, from competition to collaboration, from accumulation to illumination. Education must cease to be a mere conveyor of information and instead become an alchemy of transformation, a force that does not merely sharpen the intellect but awakens the soul.

For too long, we have mistaken education for a ladder to climb, a means to outpace others in the race for status and success. But true education is not about reaching the summit alone; it is about discovering the mountain itself—learning to read the patterns in the clouds, to feel the pulse of the earth beneath our feet, to understand that the path is not meant to be conquered but experienced. It is about seeing beyond the narrow corridors of personal ambition into the vast, intricate web of existence, where every insight gained, every skill honed, every truth uncovered is a thread in the collective tapestry of humanity.

Imagine an education that does not teach subjects in isolation but reveals the symphony of their interconnectedness. A curriculum where science does not stand apart from philosophy, where mathematics echoes the rhythms of nature, where history is not just a record of events but an unfolding of the human spirit, where art is not relegated to the margins but recognized as the language of the soul. Imagine classrooms where the ultimate lesson is not merely what to think but how to perceive—how to grasp the invisible connections that bind all knowledge into a single, living whole.

If we align our education with the deeper truth of our sacred interconnectedness—if we recognize that the mind and the heart, the intellect and the spirit, the individual and the collective are not separate but reflections of the same divine current—then learning will cease to be a race and become a revelation. No longer will knowledge be hoarded like currency, no longer will achievement be measured in isolation. Instead, education will become a force of integration, of harmony, of remembering that we are not fragments adrift in an indifferent universe, but luminous sparks of the same eternal fire.

This is the transformation we must seek—not simply a restructuring of schools, but a restructuring of consciousness. Not merely a new way of teaching, but a new way of seeing. When education reflects this universal truth—when it becomes a mirror through which we recognize ourselves in all things—it will no longer be a tool of separation, but a bridge to enlightenment.

The Essential Question

The evidence is undeniable. Across the world, we see the fractures deepening—between nations, between communities, between individuals. We grow more divided, more entrenched in our separateness, more lost in the illusion that we exist as isolated beings, disconnected from one another. Emotionally, we are hardening, drawing lines where once there was openness, retreating into self-interest where once there was a sense of belonging. The rising tides of anger, violence, and disregard for our shared humanity are no longer anomalies; they are reflections of a world that has lost sight of its inherent unity.

We misinterpret the symptoms, pointing fingers at politics, religion, race, ideology—failing to see that these are not the disease but the manifestations of a deeper wound: our estrangement from the truth of our shared origin and indivisible nature. The education we receive, the narratives we are told, the structures we uphold—all reinforce the notion that we are separate, that life is a competition, that the self must be defined in opposition to the other. We have mistaken division for reality, when in truth, it is merely the shadow cast by our own limited perception.

But shadows can be dispersed. Illusions can be unlearned. And the luminous thread of our shared heritage—though veiled—can never be extinguished. What we need is not mere reform, but a revolution of perception. A return to the core truth of existence—that we are not islands, but waves of the same ocean, branches of the same tree, notes in the same eternal song. Only when we recognize this can we break free from the false narratives that pit us against one another. Only then can we dissolve the illusions that have kept us bound to cycles of conflict and separation.

But to truly see this, we must dare to unlearn. We must dismantle the walls that education has built around our understanding, walls that tell us that intellect and wisdom are separate, that science and spirituality do not speak the same language, that one person's rise must mean another's fall. We must shatter these illusions and step into the vast, infinite landscape of truth—the truth that what we do to another, we do to ourselves; that knowledge is not ownership, but stewardship; that wisdom is not acquired, but remembered.

And so, we must ask: Can education be the bedrock of true transformation? Can it transcend mere survival and the pursuit of material success? Can it become the bridge that guides us home—to ourselves, to one another, and to the boundless mystery of existence waiting to be rediscovered?

This is the crossroads at which we stand. One path leads deeper into fragmentation, into an ever-narrowing spiral of division and self-interest. The other leads to wholeness—to an education that does not separate but unites, does not imprison but liberates, does not prepare us merely to succeed, but to become.

The choice is before us. Do we continue wandering further into the mirage of separation, or do we finally awaken to the truth of our interconnected destiny? The answer lies ahead, as we step into the next chapter: "My Journey Through the Two Paths of Education."

Chapter 7

My Journey Through the Two
Paths of Education

The pursuit of knowledge is often depicted as a steady ascent—a ladder leading ever upward, rung by rung, toward success, stability, and self-betterment. It is a story told to children, a promise embedded within the walls of every classroom: study hard, achieve more, and fulfillment will follow. Yet beneath this familiar narrative lies a deeper, unspoken truth—one that few pause to consider.

At the crossroads of education, we stand before two distinct paths, each leading to a profoundly different understanding of learning and of life itself. The first, which most of us unknowingly follow, leads ever deeper into fragmentation, reinforcing the illusion of separateness. It is a path where knowledge is not a force of unity but a tool of division—where learning becomes a race, a relentless pursuit of outshining, outperforming, and outranking. In this paradigm, education ceases to be about wisdom and understanding; instead, it becomes a means of self-advancement, a currency to be hoarded for status, security, and validation.

This is an education that mirrors the larger structures of society, conditioning us to see life as a competition rather than a collaboration. It teaches us to measure our worth not by the depth of our insight, but by the breadth of our accomplishments. It convinces us that success is found not in the expansion of our understanding, but in the accumulation of external markers of achievement. And so, we become trapped in a cycle—pursuing degrees, titles, and recognition, believing that these will bring fulfillment, only to find them fleeting, their satisfaction dissolving as soon as they are attained.

It is a path where the guiding question is not "What am I here to give?" but rather, "What's in it for me?"

I, too, walked this path for much of my early life, driven by an unquenchable thirst for achievement. Like so many others, I equated success with recognition, knowledge with superiority, learning with a means to an end. Yet as I climbed higher, accumulating accolades and accomplishments, I found that these rewards were like mirages in the desert—shimmering illusions that vanished the moment I reached for them.

The First Path: A Personal Journey

I was born in Rajasthan, India—a land of vibrant culture, deep history, and timeless traditions, but also one bound by rigid expectations. From the moment I entered the world, my future had been carefully mapped out, etched in the quiet ambitions of my loving yet traditional parents. My mother envisioned me as a doctor, my father saw me as an engineer. Their dreams were woven from love, their hopes built upon the foundations of security and stability. Yet within these carefully laid plans, my own voice struggled to be heard.

From the time I could dream, I longed to fly—not metaphorically, not in pursuit of status or success, but in the most literal sense. I wanted to be a pilot. I wanted to break free from the weight of the earth, to soar beyond boundaries, to touch the sky itself. The idea of navigating the open expanse of the heavens, of drifting above the world untethered, filled me with a longing I could neither name nor explain. But this dream was met with swift and unwavering rejection. Becoming a pilot was deemed impractical, risky, and far beyond the realm of consideration. It did not fit within the carefully constructed blueprint of success that had been drawn for me.

And so, like countless children before me, I surrendered my dream. I stepped onto the path that had been prepared, suppressing the quiet ache of unfulfilled longing, convincing myself that it was the right thing to do.

At the Birla Institute of Technology and Science, I pursued a Bachelor of Science degree. Though resigned to this course, I discovered something unexpected—a quiet passion hidden beneath layers of obligation. Chemistry, particularly organic chemistry, ignited something within me. To many of my peers, the subject was an arduous maze of formulas and memorization, a series of facts to be conquered and stored away. But to me, it was poetry in motion— an intricate dance of molecules and reactions, revealing the hidden rhythms of nature.

One professor in particular transformed my understanding. He urged us to move beyond rote memorization, to seek the why behind every equation, to perceive chemistry not as a rigid discipline but as a language—the language through which the universe itself speaks. I vividly remember the moment he posed a particularly challenging question in class and directed it toward me. A flicker of panic, then a deep breath. I let go of fear, let go of doubt, and simply understood. The answer came to me with a clarity I had never known before. In that moment, my relationship with learning changed—it was no longer about grades or performance, but about the pure joy of discovery, about unraveling the mysteries woven into the fabric of existence.

And yet, even as I pursued my master's degree and later a PhD in Polymer Technology, I remained tethered to a question that had quietly followed me through every step of my journey: "What's in it for me?" My hunger for knowledge was real, but my motivations remained rooted in ambition, in the pursuit of recognition, in the validation of success as the world defined it. I was still following the first path—believing that fulfillment was something to be acquired rather than something to be given.

A Dream Deferred and Rekindled

Beneath my academic pursuits lay a dream—one that had taken root long before I understood its weight. I was eight years old when my uncle gifted me a calendar filled with images of America—a land of towering skylines, endless highways, and boundless possibility. I remember flipping through its glossy pages, mesmerized by landscapes so different from my own, my imagination set ablaze by the promise they seemed to hold.

"One day," I told my father with the unwavering certainty only a child possesses, "I'll live there and start my own business."

That dream became my silent companion, a whisper that followed me through the years, shaping my choices in ways I did not always realize. And then, years later, it materialized. I was accepted into a PhD program at the University of Akron in Ohio, a world-renowned institution for polymer chemistry. Arriving in America felt like stepping into the pages of that childhood calendar, as though I had crossed an invisible threshold between imagination and reality.

And yet, standing in the very land I had once longed for, I felt an unexpected hollowness. I thrived academically, excelling in my research, yet something vital remained just out of reach. The work was impressive in scope, technically sound, and intellectually demanding—but it lacked the pulse of meaning. It was an exercise in precision, not passion. I had followed the path I believed would lead me to fulfillment, only to find that achievement, without a deeper sense of purpose, felt empty.

Then, life intervened. Dolly, my wife and steadfast partner in every dream, became pregnant. Suddenly, the pursuit of passion gave way to the necessity of stability. Theoretical research, with its slow and uncertain rewards, no longer seemed practical. I had to act. I had to build something tangible, something real.

In a moment of boldness, I did something unconventional—I placed an advertisement in a local newspaper, showcasing my skills and expertise. It was an act of both faith and defiance, a willingness to step outside the traditional routes to success. That decision led me to Hal Parks, a small business owner, who saw potential in what I had to offer.

The pay was modest, but the experience was invaluable. For the first time, I wasn't just a student or a researcher—I was inside the beating heart of a business. The thrill of creation, of seeing an idea take shape beyond the pages of a textbook, was intoxicating. Within months, I developed a successful product. But success does not always lead to harmony.

Tensions soon arose. Hal and I saw the world through different lenses—where I saw boundless opportunity, he saw risk. Where I wanted to push forward, he preferred to hold back. We were traveling the same road, but we were not headed toward the same destination. In time, I made the painful decision to walk away.

I stepped into my next venture—a partnership in HSH Enterprise, hoping to find alignment in shared ownership. But once again, conflicting priorities surfaced, pulling us in opposite directions. The realization dawned upon me with startling clarity: I could no longer shape my dreams within the boundaries of someone else's vision.

And so, I took the final leap—alone. In that moment of risk and resolve, POLY-CARB was born. At last, my childhood vision of building something of my own had taken form. The foundations had been laid, and for a moment, I allowed myself to believe that dreams, once realized, would sustain themselves.

But dreams alone are not enough. Reality demands more. Soon, the weight of running a company bore down on me, relentless and unyielding. Despite my unwavering ambition, despite the countless hours and tireless pursuit, the business faltered.

The vision that had once burned so brightly began to flicker, struggling against the winds of hardship. The dream that had carried me across oceans now stood at the edge of collapse, threatening to become yet another unfinished chapter in my life.

The Turning Point: Discovering the Second Path

Amid the wreckage of my business struggles, I found myself standing at a threshold—one that would either lead to my undoing or my transformation. The weight of looming failure pressed against my chest, a relentless force that shadowed my every step. Each day felt like a battle against the inevitable, an exhausting dance with uncertainty. And then, on a seemingly unremarkable Friday afternoon, the moment arrived—not with a crash, not with a grand revelation, but with the quiet, methodical unfolding of fate.

My attorney and accountant entered my office, their expressions composed, their hands clutching the documents they believed would free me from the storm. "We've prepared everything for Chapter 11 bankruptcy," they said with a practiced ease, sliding the papers across my desk. "All we need is your signature."

They spoke with the confidence of men who had seen countless others in my position, who had guided struggling business owners through this same process, time and time again. To them, bankruptcy was not failure—it was a tool, a reset button, a well-worn path to salvaging what remained. "We'll settle your debts for pennies on the dollar and save you millions, all without interrupting the business," they assured me. Their words were wrapped in reason, their logic irrefutable. And yet, as I sat there, staring at the papers before me, something deep inside me stirred—something beyond reason, beyond calculation. It was not anger, nor panic—but a quiet rising of inner knowing, subtle yet powerful, like the first whisper of dawn against the night.

I did not respond immediately. Instead, I inhaled deeply and said, with a calmness even I had not anticipated, "Let me sit with this over the weekend. I will reflect, and by Monday, I will come back to you." They nodded—expecting, perhaps, that I simply needed time to accept the inevitable. But I knew, even then, that something profound had already begun to shift within me.

Over that weekend, in the stillness of reflection, a clarity emerged—not born from analysis, but from remembrance. The weight I had carried for so long—the pressure, the fear, the endless chase for survival—began to lift. In its place arose a certainty, ancient and unshakable, something that had always been there, waiting beneath the noise.

When Monday arrived, I stepped into my office not with hesitation, but with quiet conviction.

"There isn't going to be any bankruptcy filing," I said, my voice steady, resolute. The room fell into a heavy silence. They exchanged puzzled glances, searching my face for some hidden explanation—a sudden investor, a secret reserve, some external rescue. My attorney leaned forward, furrowing his brow. "Did you find some money?" he asked, his voice edged with disbelief. I shook my head, a calm smile resting upon my lips. "No," I said simply. "But I found something far more valuable—a treasure that never expires and only grows. It's called Oneness."

In that moment, everything changed. The choice had been made—not through external rescue, but through inner alignment. And though I could not yet see the path ahead, I knew I had stepped onto sacred ground: the Second Path, where wisdom replaces fear, where purpose dissolves limitation, and where the true wealth of existence reveals itself—not in numbers, but in connection, alignment, and living truth.

The Second Path: The Power of ONENESS

Standing at the precipice of bankruptcy, I saw my reality with a starkness that stripped away every illusion I had ever clung to. The vision of success I had chased for so long—shaped by ambition, recognition, and the pursuit of external validation—now lay before me like a mirage dissolving in the heat. What I had believed to be achievement was, in truth, an empty shell, a pursuit that had distanced me not only from others but from myself. My business struggles were not merely financial; they were the manifestation of something deeper, something broken at the very core of my being.

As I sat in my office that Friday afternoon, surrounded by the weight of my failures, with the bankruptcy documents laid before me, the familiar voice of survival urged me to act, to sign, to escape.

But somewhere deeper, a quieter voice—the voice of knowing—asked me to pause. And so I did.

"Let me sit with this over the weekend," I said, surprising even myself. "I will come back to you on Monday." It was not an act of strategy; it was a sacred postponement—a silent prayer for clarity beyond the noise of fear.

Over that weekend, in the stillness of reflection, the words of my mother, a woman of quiet wisdom and unshakable faith, rose into my heart like a lost melody returning home. She had once told me: "There are two paths to success: the path of knowledge and the path of wisdom. Knowledge is valuable, but it is limited. It teaches you how to achieve, but not how to sustain or find peace. Wisdom, on the other hand, reveals the deeper truths of life and leads to fulfillment."

At the time, I had nodded, absorbing her words with the detached curiosity of someone too young to grasp their full weight. But now, as I stood on the edge of losing everything, their meaning unfurled before me with undeniable clarity. Knowledge had led me here—to achievement, to ambition, to a company I had built with relentless drive. But wisdom? Wisdom had eluded me.

She often spoke of Oneness—the eternal, unbreakable truth that all existence is woven by a single thread, an invisible current flowing through every being, every breath. My mother, a devoted reader of the world's sacred texts—the Bhagavad Gita, the Bible, the Quran, the Guru Granth Sahib—carried in her heart a quiet fire of spiritual knowing. It was through her voice that I first heard the sacred resonance of Ik Onkaar—Guru Nanak's unveiling of the truth that we are not isolated fragments, but emanations of one divine source. In time, her words ceased to be mere teachings; they became revelation. She had tried to tell me that true success is not measured by what we acquire, but by what we align with. That the pursuit of self-interest leads only to fragmentation—but through the remembrance of Oneness, life's deepest truths are revealed.

In search of further guidance, I reached for a worn book of quotes that had sat untouched on my shelf for years. I flipped through its pages, and my eyes landed on the words of Albert Einstein:

"A person experiences life as something separate from the rest—a kind of optical delusion of consciousness. Our task must be to free ourselves from this self-imposed prison and, through compassion, to find the reality of Oneness."

The words struck me like lightning, cutting through the fog of my despair. I understood, with a certainty beyond logic, why I had failed. My business had been built on a fractured foundation—on the illusion of separation, the misguided belief that success was something to be won, rather than something to be shared. I had led a vast team of highly educated individuals, yet the collective mindset—unspoken but deeply ingrained—revolved around a single question: "What's in it for me?" And so, without realizing it, I had cultivated an environment where individuals worked in silos, where competition replaced collaboration, where survival took precedence over service.

Oneness, I now realized, was not some abstract philosophy, nor a distant spiritual ideal—it was a fundamental truth, as real and as necessary as breath itself. It was the understanding that we are not islands, adrift in a sea of isolation, but threads in a single, boundless tapestry. It was the recognition that just as a thousand lightbulbs draw their power from the same unseen current, so too do all living beings draw life from a shared, universal energy.

And in that moment of awakening, I knew: If I was to rebuild, if I was to transform my life and my business, it would not be through strategy alone. Not through financial maneuvers or clever marketing. It would be through alignment—with something far greater than myself, with the pulse of Oneness that hums through every leaf, every soul, and every breath of creation.

The road ahead was uncertain, but for the first time, I was not afraid. The path had revealed itself—not the one shaped by the mask of ambition, nor the one driven by self-interest, but the one where success was no longer an isolated pursuit, but a shared awakening. And with that sacred knowing, I stepped forward.

Transforming POLY-CARB: Building a Business on ONENESS

In that defining moment, I knew that POLY-CARB could not simply persist as it was. This was not a crisis of spreadsheets, nor a mere test of strategic agility. It was something far more profound—a reckoning with the very spirit that had shaped its foundations. A business, much like a living being, is imbued with the essence of those who build it. Mine had been sculpted from the hardened clay of ambition, erected on pillars of self-interest, and unknowingly distanced from the very principles that sustain true growth. It had sought expansion without alignment, progress without meaning, and in doing so, had drifted further from its highest potential. But now, as clarity cut through the haze of past illusions, I saw the undeniable truth: if POLY-CARB was to endure—not merely to survive but to thrive—it had to be reborn. It could no longer exist as an isolated entity chasing profit; it had to become a living manifestation of Oneness itself.

With this realization came a painful yet necessary decision—I had to tell my team the truth: we were broke, and salaries could no longer be paid. They were good, diligent individuals, yet they had been shaped by the very transactional mindset that had brought us to this precipice. Their relationship to work was tethered to personal gain, measured through the narrow prism of competition and self-preservation, where success was defined not by connection, but by conquest. When faced with the reality that there were no more financial guarantees, most of them chose to leave—not out of malice, but because the foundation they stood upon had crumbled. And I understood. They had been trained to chase security, not purpose.

But what I was about to build required something entirely different. It demanded minds unshackled from convention, hearts unburdened by the weight of hierarchy, and spirits free from the rigid machinery of profit-driven enterprise. I sought out fresh thinkers— young, unguarded souls who had not yet been conditioned to see work as mere survival, but who could still glimpse it as an act of service, creation, and shared destiny. What I was assembling was not a team in the conventional sense, but a collective—one that would redefine the very fabric of work itself.

From the very beginning, we wove something unprecedented into existence. POLY-CARB was no longer a mere company; it became an organism, pulsing with intention, flowing with a sense of purpose beyond the confines of traditional business. It was no longer confined to profit margins and market share—it had a soul, a heartbeat that resonated with something far greater.

There were no rigid hierarchies, no ornamental titles, no compartments dictating who could contribute and who could not. Leadership was no longer an emblem of status but a living force, an energy that flowed through each and every member, guiding decisions not through authority, but through wisdom and shared responsibility.

Weekly gatherings became sacred rituals—not the sterile, perfunctory meetings of corporate culture, but spaces of reflection and realignment. These were moments where we did not just discuss strategy or evaluate performance; we asked deeper questions. Why were we here? What were we creating—not in terms of products, but in terms of impact, meaning, and contribution? Were we merely operating a company, or were we cultivating something far greater—a movement, a philosophy, a revolution in how business could exist in harmony with the whole?

Decisions were no longer driven by profit alone but by a guiding principle that resonated through every aspect of our work: How does this serve the whole? We began to see that financial success was not an end, but a natural consequence of integrity, alignment, and purpose. Departments no longer guarded knowledge like treasures locked away in silos. The invisible walls of competition, once reinforced by fear of irrelevance, crumbled. In their place emerged a dynamic, fluid ecosystem—one where engineers collaborated seamlessly with marketers, where customer service wove insights directly into product development, where ideas moved without obstruction. Trust, once an afterthought in a system built on control, became the very fabric that held us together.

The transformation was not without its trials. The old ghosts of competition and insecurity lingered in the corridors, whispering that survival demanded aggression, that kindness was weakness, that hierarchy ensured order. But we chose another path. We reminded ourselves daily that we were not here to chase market dominance, nor to build an empire atop the brittle bones of a self that had forgotten its source. We were here to create something that would outlast us, something that would ripple beyond the boundaries of a balance sheet—a living testament to the power of Oneness in action.

And as we embraced this new paradigm, something extraordinary happened. The very air within POLY-CARB changed. Employees who had once viewed their roles as mere obligations now arrived with purpose, not because they had to, but because they wanted to. Job descriptions dissolved into something more fluid, more alive. People were not just workers; they were creators, catalysts of transformation. Ideas flourished—not because they were incentivized, but because they were valued, because they mattered. Our products, once just functional solutions, became something greater—they became expressions of our philosophy, designed with intention, with heart, with a commitment to serve beyond the bottom line.

Customers felt the shift. They were no longer engaging with a faceless entity, an impersonal supplier of goods. They were engaging with something that resonated, something that felt different—an ethos, a way of being. Our interactions were no longer mere transactions; they became relationships, exchanges built on trust, on mutual respect, on shared purpose. And as word spread, our impact expanded.

Within a few short years, POLY-CARB emerged from the shadows of failure into a thriving success story. But the numbers, the revenue, the market recognition—these were not the real markers of triumph. The true victory lay in the quiet moments—the unspoken trust that wove us together, the way we saw one another not as employees but as co-creators of something profound. We had not just built a business. We had built a movement.

The world began to take notice. Our story spread, attracting partnerships, opening doors that had once seemed beyond reach. Yet, through it all, POLY-CARB remained what it had become—a living testament to the power of Oneness. It stood as proof that when collaboration, compassion, and a shared sense of purpose take precedence over ego, the results extend far beyond financial success. They create something far more valuable—a culture, a legacy, a reminder that business, at its highest form, is not about what we take, but about what we give.

The Question That Changed Everything

At the heart of this transformation was a single, profound question: "What am I here to give?" It was this shift—from accumulation to contribution—that changed everything. Before this moment, like so many others, we had operated under a very different question "What's in it for me?" This mindset is embedded in us from an early age, reinforced through education and by a world that equates success with what we take rather than what we offer. But this new question turned the paradigm on its head.

It was no longer about building a business for personal achievement. It was about creating something that served, uplifted, and contributed to the world in a meaningful way. This one shift in thinking ignited a ripple effect. My leadership changed, my team's motivation changed, and ultimately, the very trajectory of POLY-CARB changed.

We were no longer striving to be the biggest or the most profitable—we were striving to be of the greatest service. And ironically, in doing so, success followed effortlessly.

A New Perspective on Leadership

This realization unraveled everything I had once believed about leadership. I had spent years convinced that a leader's purpose was to command, to strategize, to maintain control with precision and foresight. Leadership, as I had understood it, was about standing at the helm, steering the ship, ensuring that every move was calculated for success. But now, I saw the flaw in this thinking. True leadership was not about being at the top—it was about being at the center, not as a ruler, but as a guide, holding space for others to grow, create, and thrive.

I no longer saw myself as the head of a company, but as the steward of an ecosystem—one that required balance, nourishment, and alignment rather than rigid control. My role was not to dictate outcomes but to serve—to remove barriers that hindered growth, to cultivate a culture of trust, and to encourage each individual to step into their highest potential. Leadership was no longer about power; it was about empowerment. It was not about commanding results; it was about inspiring purpose.

When leadership is rooted in Oneness, it transcends the traditional frameworks of authority and hierarchy. It ceases to be about managing people and instead becomes an act of awakening—the awakening of potential, of vision, of purpose. It becomes a practice of reminding others of the truth that had so profoundly transformed me: that life is not measured by what we extract from the world, but by what we contribute to it. Leadership, at its purest, is not about directing the course—it is about illuminating the path.

The Power of Purpose-Driven Innovation

The principles of Oneness and the guiding question, "What am I here to give?," did not remain confined within the walls of POLY-CARB. They became the very essence of how we engaged with the world— reshaping not only our internal culture but also our interactions with customers, partners, and even competitors.

Where once we had viewed rival companies as obstacles to outmaneuver, we now saw them as fellow travelers on the same journey. Instead of hoarding information in the name of competitive advantage, we shared insights freely. Instead of operating from a mindset of scarcity, we sought opportunities for collaboration, recognizing that true innovation does not emerge from isolation, but from the merging of perspectives, talents, and ideas.

This shift in mindset opened doors we had never even thought to knock on. Partnerships formed where competition had once stood. Conversations that might have been guarded and strategic became open and generative. And as we aligned ourselves with a higher purpose—not just to succeed, but to serve—our impact expanded in ways we could not have anticipated.

But the transformation did not stop with the business. It became deeply personal. The philosophy of Oneness wove itself into the lives of those who had embraced it, shaping their relationships, their communities, and their aspirations. Many of my team members carried this perspective into their personal worlds, seeing the ripple effect of contribution in ways far beyond their work at POLY-CARB. Some went on to start businesses of their own, infused with the same principles of unity, integrity, and service.

And so, the true legacy of POLY-CARB was never just in its products, its revenue, or its market success. It was in the spirit of Oneness that continued to spread—beyond boardrooms and balance sheets, beyond industry and competition, into the very fabric of how we live, create, and lead.

The Legacy of ONENESS: Beyond Business

When POLY-CARB was acquired by DOW Chemical Co. in 2007, it marked the close of one chapter but the dawn of another. For many, such an acquisition would be measured solely in financial terms—a culmination of ambition, a testament to years of perseverance. But for me, it was something far greater. It was an affirmation that the path we had walked, guided by the spirit of giving, was not just an idealistic pursuit, but a model that could be both sustainable and scalable. It was proof that success did not have to come at the cost of purpose, that integrity and impact were not mere luxuries but the very foundations of enduring prosperity.

Yet, even as I stepped away from POLY-CARB, I knew that my journey was far from over. A single question had begun to take root within me, one that expanded far beyond the realm of business: If Oneness could transform a company, could it not also transform education, leadership, and even society itself?

This realization became the catalyst for my next mission. The wisdom that had redefined my understanding of business was never meant to be confined—it was far too vast, far too essential to remain tethered to any single industry. It was not just a principle; it was a way of being, a blueprint for a world shaped by harmony, purpose, and deeper connection.

And so, my purpose evolved. I no longer sought to build another company—I sought to build something far more enduring: a movement, a shift in consciousness, a call to those ready to lead not with ambition, but with alignment; not with authority, but with authenticity. My work became about sharing what I had discovered—not just about business, but about the art of living, creating, and leading from a place of unity. It took shape through my books, lectures, programs, television shows, and a weekly radio show that has remained on air for over 25 years, touching lives across generations.

A Call to Action: Building a Future on Giving

As I reflect on this journey, one reality emerges with absolute clarity—Oneness and the mindset of giving are not merely principles for a meaningful life or a thriving business; they are the missing foundation stones of our education system. They are what we have forgotten in our pursuit of knowledge, in our race for achievement, in our relentless march toward individual success.

For too long, we have conditioned students to compete, to achieve, to accumulate, but what if we instead prepared them to give, to collaborate, to uplift? What if we replaced the question "What's in it for me?" with the far more powerful "What am I here to give?"

Imagine a world where classrooms are no longer confined to the mere transmission of facts but instead become sanctuaries of wisdom, empathy, and interconnectedness. Where students graduate not just with degrees, but with a profound sense of purpose—their unique gift to the world, their place within the greater whole. Imagine an education that does not merely equip individuals to navigate the world as isolated beings but inspires them to contribute to it, to nurture it, to weave themselves into its intricate and boundless fabric.

This is the true legacy of our journey—a reminder that real transformation does not begin outside of us; it begins within. The moment we shift from taking to giving, from separateness to unity, from vanity to purpose, we awaken a force far greater than ourselves. We step into the vast, uncharted space where wisdom flourishes, where learning is no longer about amassing knowledge but about embodying understanding.

If we are to truly transform society, we must begin by reimagining education—not as a system that prepares students for competition, but as a vehicle that fosters unity, service, and shared purpose. We must create a path that does not merely teach information but illuminates the profound connections that bind us all. This is how we build a future where individuals no longer see themselves as isolated fragments but as integral threads within the vast and beautiful tapestry of existence.

Chapter 8

The Path of Wisdom to Education

The path of wisdom is not a destination; it is a homecoming—a return to the eternal truth that has always pulsed at the heart of existence. It is a path not paved with competition or conquest, but with clarity, purpose, and reverence for the whole. At its core lies the understanding that a single, boundless Universal Power animates all life—unfettered by the illusions of race, nationality, gender, or any of the fleeting labels we impose upon ourselves.

Our physical forms are temporary vessels, mere spacesuits housing this infinite energy. But when we mistake the vessel for the essence, we imprison ourselves in the limitations of fear, greed, and ego, cutting ourselves off from the great current of wisdom that flows through all things. To walk the path of wisdom is to shed this illusion—to see beyond the shell and recognize the shared light within.

When our minds are guided not by the narrow constraints of self-interest but by the rhythm of Universal Truth, we awaken to a new way of being. The relentless hunger for external validation fades, replaced by an unwavering gratitude—a desire to learn, to evolve, not for personal gain but as an offering to something far greater than ourselves.

Yet, to step onto this path, we must first cultivate awareness—an unflinching willingness to confront the illusions that bind us. Wisdom is not found in accumulating knowledge, but in aligning ourselves with the eternal symphony of existence. And when we do, knowledge is no longer something we possess—it is something we become.

The Body as a Metaphor for Humanity

To understand the catastrophic consequences of separation, let us turn to a metaphor—the human body as a mirror of humanity itself.

The body is an orchestration of miracles—an intricate web of organs, tissues, and cells, each performing its own sacred function while remaining inseparably connected to the whole. When one part ails, the entire system suffers. If we consume something toxic, the damage is not confined to a single organ; the distress ripples throughout, affecting every cell, every breath. In short, the body remains healthy only when all its components work together in harmony.

But imagine if, through an unprecedented breakthrough, scientists developed nanochips—advanced microprocessors capable of independent thought. These chips are implanted in every part of the body: the hands, the feet, the heart, the lungs, the brain. Now, each body part has its own intelligence, its own free will, its own agenda.

At first, the system functions seamlessly. Each component works efficiently, making decisions that appear beneficial for itself. But over time, something shifts. The hands grow resentful, believing they do more work than the feet. The heart starts complaining that the brain takes all the credit. The legs refuse to move unless they receive additional recognition. Each part, now guided by self-interest rather than unity, begins to pursue its own separate agenda.

What was once a harmonious whole descends into dysfunction. The body collapses—not because its individual parts lacked intelligence, but because they lost sight of their shared purpose.

The Tale of Charlie and the Nanochips

At a prestigious biomedical research institute, a team of visionary scientists engineered a groundbreaking nanochip—an innovation capable of mirroring the intricate workings of the human brain. This marvel of technology could learn, adapt, and even simulate emotions with uncanny precision. To push the boundaries of their creation, they selected Charlie as their perfect test subject, embedding a nanochip into each of his vital organs and limbs, transforming him into a living symphony of human biology and artificial intelligence.

Man and machine briefly aligned. Charlie became a remarkable fusion of human and bionic technology. Each of his body parts functioned with enhanced efficiency, making independent decisions while maintaining harmony. But then, the fractures began to appear.

One day, Charlie decided to drive to the mall. As he buckled his seatbelt, his stomach—now an independent thinker—grumbled in protest, complaining that the belt was far too tight. Charlie, eager to appease, loosened it. No sooner had he started the engine than his right foot began to grumble, fuming that the left foot was lounging idly while it bore the burden of acceleration.

Offended, the left foot snapped back, accusing the right foot of arrogance and self-importance.

The hands soon joined the uproar, each claiming to be the true master of the steering wheel. The lungs, feeling overlooked, demanded more oxygen, while the eyes, desperate to focus on the road ahead, pleaded for unity. But their cries were drowned in the rising cacophony of rebellion—each part of Charlie's body now operating with singular intent, blind to the greater whole.

Then, in a final act of reckless defiance, the right foot slammed down on the accelerator. The hands, still locked in their feud, lost control of the wheel. The stomach, overwhelmed by stress, twisted in knots of protest. And Charlie—once the orchestrator of his own being—became nothing more than a helpless passenger in a body that had turned against itself.

The car veered wildly, swerving across the road before crashing into a tree. When Charlie awoke in the hospital, his body was fractured—not by an outside force, but by the war within, by the chaos born from division, by the simple yet devastating truth: a system that turns against itself cannot survive.

A Metaphor for Humanity

Charlie's story is our story—the story of a world fractured by the same forces that tore his body apart. Like Charlie's limbs, we were designed to work in unity—interconnected, interdependent, thriving together. Yet, somewhere along the way, we allowed the illusion of separateness to take hold. Instead of seeing ourselves as parts of a greater whole, we became fixated on individual interests, territorial boundaries, and competitive pursuits.

The consequences of this fragmentation extend beyond politics and economics—they seep into every facet of existence. From environmental destruction to mental health crises, from social injustice to inner turmoil, we are witnessing the unraveling of a system that was never meant to function in isolation.

And at the heart of this dysfunction lies a fundamental flaw: the way we educate ourselves and future generations.

Toward a Transformative Education

If we are to heal the fractures within our world, we must begin with the way we learn. The solution is not merely to reform education, but to redefine it—to shift from a model that teaches competition and accumulation to one that fosters wisdom, collaboration, and shared purpose.

Education must move beyond the rote transmission of facts and formulas. It must become a sanctuary for insight, emotional intelligence, and self-awareness. It must teach students not what to think, but how to think—how to question, how to perceive, how to discern truth from illusion. Above all, it must awaken them to their role in something greater than themselves.

It must also embrace experiential learning—inviting students to engage with nature, diverse communities, and real-world challenges, where curiosity is kindled, empathy is deepened, and resilience is forged. When education is rooted in the truth of our shared humanity, it produces individuals who rise above prejudice, see beyond borders, and make decisions not from fear, but from wisdom.

This transformative path does not aim to produce workers—it seeks to nurture creators, visionaries, and compassionate leaders. It does not ask, "How will you compete?" but instead, "How will you contribute?" It replaces the question, "What's in it for me?" with the soul's calling, "What am I here to give?"

This is the wisdom path of education—a path that does not fragment, but unites; that does not isolate, but illuminates; that does not prepare us merely to succeed—but to become.

The Journey Inward

And yet, if we are to truly embrace this path, we must begin with an essential question—one that has echoed through the ages, waiting for each of us to answer in our own time:

Who am I?

For without self-knowledge, how can we understand the nature of existence? How can we awaken to the deeper truths that lie beyond illusion? How can we step into a life of wisdom, purpose, and connection?

In the next chapter, we embark upon this most fundamental of inquiries—the journey inward, where the greatest transformation of all begins.

Chapter 9

Who Am I? The Path to Self-Knowledge

To truly grasp the transformative power of self-knowledge, one must first confront a disquieting truth: the beliefs we cherish—our values, judgments, decisions, and even our sense of purpose—are often built upon a fractured and fragmented understanding of reality. The mind, filtering existence through the narrow aperture of individual perception, rarely touches the immutable and eternal truths that lie beyond the fleeting world of forms.

From the moment we draw our first breath, we are entrusted with a singular and intricate vessel—a biological masterpiece, self-sustaining and ever-adapting. This body, the carrier of our earthly experience, arrives unmarked, yet is swiftly adorned with labels: gender, race, nationality, religion. These identities, inherited from lineage and circumstance, become the scaffolding upon which we construct our understanding of self. A name is given, further solidifying our presence within the boundaries of societal expectation. And so, the body becomes the anchor of our existence, the lens through which we navigate the world.

Within this miraculous vessel resides a formidable instrument—the brain—a computational marvel capable of extraordinary feats of logic, creativity, and introspection. Equipped with five senses, it gathers an incessant stream of data from the external world, sculpting our understanding of reality. Yet herein lies the paradox: the knowledge acquired through these senses is inherently incomplete, a mosaic of unverified impressions that form the foundation of our worldview.

As we journey through life, this sensory data accumulates, layering upon itself like sediment settling in a riverbed. The narratives imparted by parents, teachers, and culture reinforce this constructed reality, embedding within us the belief that we are solely our bodies—confined to the limits of what we can see, hear, and touch. This illusion weaves itself so seamlessly into our consciousness that we mistake it for truth, fostering a sense of separateness and alienation from the greater whole.

To transcend this illusion, we must embark upon a path of self-inquiry, guided by one of the most ancient and profound questions: "Who am I?" This is not merely a philosophical exercise—it is an unraveling, a peeling away of conditioned thought and inherited assumptions. It is a quest to unearth the truth that lies beyond form, beyond identity, beyond the veils of illusion. In the stillness of this inquiry, we begin to sense the golden thread of universal wisdom that interlaces all of existence.

Awakening to the Truth

True self-knowledge is not confined to introspection alone; it is an awakening, a realignment with the fundamental and unwavering truths that underlie creation itself. It is a recognition that we are not merely our bodies, nor the labels assigned to us, nor the fleeting experiences that shape our perceptions. Rather, we are the eternal consciousness that animates this existence, boundless and indivisible.

To remain tethered to the belief that we are only our physical form is to be held hostage by the fragility and impermanence of the body. This identification breeds an unrelenting fear—fear of loss, of inadequacy, of the inevitable passage of time. It fuels an insatiable thirst for self-preservation, compelling us into an endless pursuit of validation, success, and accumulation, as if by achieving more, acquiring more, or controlling more, we might somehow defy the inevitable. Yet, no matter how much we build, how fiercely we grasp, or how high we climb—the body remains acutely aware of its finite nature—keeping us locked in cycles of longing, insecurity, and ego-driven separation.

But the moment we summon the courage to step beyond the veil of illusion, to turn inward and ask with unshakable sincerity, "Who am I"—beneath this name, within this body, and untouched by the passing tide of existence?—the shroud of forgetfulness begins to lift. The mirage of separateness fades, dissolving into the vast expanse of truth that has awaited us since the beginning of time. And in that sacred awakening, we do not become something new—we return to what we have always been: infinite, indestructible, and luminous beyond measure.

The Allegory of the Spacesuits

Imagine an era when beings of pure energy roamed freely across the boundless expanse of the universe. In their encounters, however, misunderstandings frequently arose, escalating into conflicts that threatened to unravel the fragile fabric of existence itself. To resolve this growing discord, a wise leader summoned a universal assembly, seeking a solution to bridge the divides and restore harmony.

Representatives from countless worlds converged on Earth, but an obstacle soon became apparent. These luminous beings of pure energy were incapable of perceiving one another directly, nor could they comprehend each other's languages. To address this conundrum, the greatest minds among them conceived a remarkable invention: spacesuits. These ingenious suits, specifically designed for Earth's environment, enabled the beings to interact and communicate with one another. Crafted in a dazzling variety of colors, shapes, and sizes, the suits were equipped with five senses, allowing their wearers to experience the world in profoundly new ways.

Encased within their spacesuits, the beings were enthralled by the sensations and wonders that this new mode of existence afforded them. For the first time, they could see, hear, touch, taste, and smell the world around them. The suits also carried the extraordinary ability to facilitate reproduction, enabling the creation of new life.

As eons passed, however, the beings became increasingly enraptured by their suits. What was once a tool for connection became a source of identity. They began to adorn their suits, vying with one another over their appearances, and grew so attached to these external forms that they forgot their true essence as beings of pure energy. In their forgetfulness, they mistook the suits for their ultimate selves, perpetuating the very conflicts the suits had been designed to overcome. The beings no longer recognized the unity that transcended their external forms, reigniting divisions and undermining the harmony they had once sought.

The Deeper Truth

The spacesuits in the allegory symbolize our human bodies—temporary vessels crafted to enable our journey on Earth. Yet, much like the beings in the tale, we have become captivated by the superficial, losing sight of the universal force that animates us all. We have been conditioned to define ourselves by our physicality, our external labels, and the fleeting accomplishments of the material world, neglecting the profound essence that dwells within.

Just as electricity powers lightbulbs of various shapes and colors, a singular, omnipresent energy enlivens each of us. This energy does not discriminate; it flows through all beings, animating them with life and purpose. Beneath the diversity of our external forms lies an unbroken thread of connection—a shared essence that transcends all distinctions. Despite our perceived differences, we are all manifestations of the same cosmic energy, bound together by an intrinsic unity that extends far beyond our limited understanding.

To realize this is to awaken from the illusion of separateness. It is to see that the barriers we construct—between races, religions, genders, and nations—are mere projections of a fragmented mind, a mind that has lost its awareness of the whole. When we align our consciousness with the universal truth of our sacred origins, we free ourselves from the narrow confines of ego, stepping into a life imbued with purpose, unity, and profound understanding. This is not a concept to be merely believed, but a reality to be experienced—a paradigm shift in perception that dissolves fear, rivalry, and discord, replacing them with compassion, acceptance, and peace.

This awakening redefines our perspective on knowledge, transforming it from a tool for personal advancement into a means for collective service. In the state of alignment with the universal flow, knowledge ceases to be a currency for competition and control; instead, it becomes a sacred offering, a means of illuminating the path for others. Our skills, talents, and intellect evolve into instruments of harmony and compassion, serving a greater whole. We no longer learn merely to acquire, but to contribute, to uplift, and to bridge the gaps that divide humanity.

Imagine a world where knowledge is not hoarded for personal gain, but shared freely to enrich the collective consciousness. A world where education is not confined to facts and figures but expands into wisdom that nurtures the soul, aligns the heart with truth, and fosters a deep sense of interconnectedness. In such a world, competition gives way to collaboration, ambition is tempered by humility, and progress is measured not by material wealth but by the depth of one's inner fulfillment and service to others.

Yet, for this shift to take root, we must first recognize the distractions that keep us entangled in illusions. The constant pursuit of status, wealth, and validation pulls us away from the deeper truths of existence. We build identities around transient achievements, clinging to external markers of success while ignoring the eternal wisdom that has always resided within us. It is only by turning inward, by questioning the stories we have been told, that we begin to peel away the layers of conditioning and rediscover the unchanging essence beneath.

When we understand that our existence is not limited to the physical, we transcend the fears that hold us back. The fear of mortality, of inadequacy, of failure—these dissolve in the light of deeper awareness. We come to see that our purpose is not merely to survive, to accumulate, or to dominate, but to express the highest potential of our being—to create, to love, to uplift, and to serve as conduits of the universal intelligence that moves through all things.

This is the deeper truth: we are not separate, but one. We are not here merely to exist, but to awaken. And in that awakening, we reclaim the boundless wisdom, the infinite love, and the divine interconnectedness that has been ours all along.

The Path Forward

To embrace our sacred unity is to transcend the illusion of separateness and awaken to the divine truth that every thought, word, and action sends ripples across the vast, interconnected web of existence. We are not isolated fragments adrift in a chaotic universe, but intricate threads woven into a grand cosmic tapestry— bound by the eternal flow of cause and effect, shaped by forces seen and unseen.

Yet, awakening to this truth is not enough. Awareness must lead to alignment. We must ask not only "Who am I?" but also "What impact do my actions create?" This question is not a mere abstraction—it is the very foundation upon which life unfolds.

It is here that we encounter the profound and intricate tapestry of karma—the silent architect of destiny, the unseen force sculpting our experiences, the mirror reflecting the essence of our choices. Karma is neither punishment nor reward; it is the law of harmony, the natural unfolding of energy that moves through all existence. Every action—no matter how small—leaves an imprint upon the fabric of life, reverberating across time and space.

Why must we explore this concept deeply?

Because karma is the compass of our evolution—a reminder that we are not passive recipients of fate but active participants in the great unfolding of creation. To truly embody our shared divinity, we must recognize that our lives are not mere accidents but expressions of accumulated intent, shaped by past deeds and continuously reshaped by the choices we make in each moment.

Understanding karma shifts our perspective from self-interest to service, from fleeting desires to lasting contribution. It dissolves the illusion of victimhood, replacing it with the empowering realization that we are the authors of our destiny. With this understanding, every choice becomes sacred—an opportunity to uplift, to heal, to inspire, and to serve.

The next chapter unfolds as a sacred journey into the profound path of service and karma—revealing how it serves as both a guiding force and a mirror reflecting our highest potential. We will explore how the conscious alignment of thought, intention, and action not only shapes our personal destiny but also weaves the fabric of the world's unfolding story. Through this awareness, we step into a life of fulfillment, harmony, and purposeful service—not as mere participants, but as architects of a brighter, more awakened existence.

Chapter 10

The Profound Path of Service and Karma

Like an unseen river flowing beneath the fabric of existence, karma weaves the silent, unerring architecture of our destiny. It sculpts our experiences with an artistry so intricate that few pause to perceive its guiding hand. Ancient wisdom whispers its immutable truths: "As you sow, so shall you reap. What goes around, comes around." Yet, karma, in its infinite depth, is often misinterpreted—reduced to a simplistic notion of reward and retribution.

In truth, karma is neither a celestial arbiter nor a force of reckoning; it is a mirror—reflecting with unwavering clarity the energies we cultivate, the intentions we nurture, and the choices we make. It neither punishes nor favors; it restores. Like a masterful weaver, it aligns our steps toward equilibrium, unveiling the path of self-awareness and awakening. It demands not our obedience, but invites our understanding. It imposes no suffering, yet grants us the lessons necessary to transcend it.

The Whispering Lessons of Karma

In every bond we forge, in every crossing of paths, karma speaks. It calls us to relinquish the burdens of fear, insecurity, greed, and ego, peeling away the illusions that entangle us in cycles of struggle. It beckons us back to our essence—not fragmented, not divided, but an inseparable thread in the grand, sacred fabric of existence.

To embrace karma as a gift is to step into liberation. It shatters the illusion that life happens to us, revealing instead that life unfolds through us. We are both the architects and the artisans of our fate, the composers of the symphony that reverberates through the corridors of time.

When we transition from reaction to awareness, from resistance to reverence, karma ceases to be a force to be feared and becomes a teacher to be cherished. Nothing is without purpose, no encounter is devoid of meaning, no trial is absent of wisdom. Every moment is a classroom, every experience a scripture, inscribed upon the scroll of eternity.

Yet, when we resist karma's guidance—when we cling to blame, entitlement, or victimhood—we ensnare ourselves in the very patterns we are meant to transcend. Circumstances are not injustices inflicted upon us but are echoes of the energy we have set into motion.

The Sacred Keys to Liberation

To break free from the binding cycles of karma, we must embrace three sacred keys:

1. **Gratitude** – It elevates us beyond the past, unveiling hidden lessons and inviting unseen possibilities. Gratitude shifts our perspective from lack to abundance, from hardship to wisdom, allowing us to see beyond momentary trials and embrace the deeper orchestration of our growth.

2. **Acceptance and Patience** – In relinquishing judgment and surrendering to the unfolding of life, we create space for transformation to take root. Acceptance does not mean resignation; it means understanding that every experience, no matter how difficult, serves a purpose in our evolution.

3. **Presence and Gratefulness** – By embracing each moment as sacred, even our setbacks become avenues for creativity, wisdom, and profound impact. When we are present, we become conscious participants in life's unfolding instead of passive recipients.

Service: The Embodiment of Karma

To live in harmony with karma is to remember our true nature. It is to relinquish all that no longer serves and to step forward, unshackled, into the fullness of our being. Bound to ego, we perceive ourselves as solitary sculptors of destiny, measuring life's trials through the narrow lens of personal justice. We resist, we recoil, we lament. Yet, when we shift from "What can I take?" to "What can I give?" the veil is lifted. We see ourselves no longer as isolated figures, but as divine threads interwoven in the grand, cosmic design.

In this state of service, even suffering loses its sting. Challenges cease to be burdens and become invitations—portals through which we may pour forth our wisdom, creativity, and love. Many of history's greatest innovations and triumphs were born from this perspective. I, too, have witnessed its power. During my tenure at Poly-Carb, when I shifted from a mindset of self-interest to one of contribution, a quiet alchemy unfolded. Growth and prosperity blossomed, mirroring the alignment within me. I came to see that karma is not a force of judgment—it is a compass, guiding us to pause, to reflect, to ascend to higher planes of awareness.

The Interwoven Realms of Karma

Karma is both profoundly personal and undeniably collective. It does not operate in isolation, for no soul exists in solitude. Like ripples upon a still pond, our every thought, word, and action extend outward, shaping not only our own destiny but the world itself.

A child does not arrive as a blank slate; they bear the imprints of past energies, past actions, past journeys. And beyond their own karma, they inherit the karma of their lineage—the unseen legacies of their parents, the silent energies of their home, the vibrations of the society that raises them.

So too does karma manifest in civilizations. Societies steeped in greed, division, and exploitation inevitably collapse under their own weight, while those rooted in wisdom, unity, and truth cultivate a legacy that flourishes for generations. History stands as testimony—great empires have risen through conquest, only to wither from within. But those who plant seeds of enlightenment leave behind a garden that blooms far beyond their time.

Beyond Human Notions of Justice

Many ask, why do those who cause harm seem to escape consequence? The answer lies beyond the grasp of human perception. Karma does not adhere to fleeting timelines, nor does it conform to our notions of fairness. It is not a system of punishment but a force of balance.

Gautama Buddha's wisdom pierces the veil of illusion: "Nothing ever happens to you for which you are not the cause." This truth dissolves the illusion of victimhood and unveils a profound reality—we are not passive recipients of fate, but active participants in the unfolding of our own existence.

Human laws may falter, swayed by power and privilege, but karma remains incorruptible. It does not favor the wealthy or the influential, nor does it bow to deception. It moves as the tides—silent, unseen, but inevitable. Even when outward consequences seem absent, the inner toll is inescapable. No wealth, no status, no title can silence the whisper of an unsettled conscience.

And yet, karma is not a force of retribution—it is a force of awakening. Every hardship we endure is not a condemnation, but a lesson. Every struggle is an invitation to evolve beyond the patterns that bind us, to step into a higher state of awareness.

The Journey of True Service

If nothing occurs for which we are not the cause, then the power to reshape our destiny is not in the hands of fate—it is in our own. The question is not "Why is this happening to me?" but rather, "What am I creating?" What unseen threads am I weaving into the grand tapestry of existence? What future am I sculpting with the silent force of my thoughts, the weight of my words, the imprint of my deeds?

The highest gift we can offer the world is the purest expression of our being—unburdened by ego, unshackled from fear, untethered from the illusions of self-interest. When we operate from this space, we become vessels of something greater, igniting ripples of karmic harmony that stretch far beyond our reach, uplifting lives in ways we may never witness, yet deeply feel.

And yet, education—as it exists today—often fails to illuminate this truth. It sharpens the intellect but leaves the soul yearning, adrift in a sea of external achievements that offer no true fulfillment. It equips us for professions but does not prepare us for purpose. What if learning was not merely the accumulation of knowledge, but the sacred unfolding of destiny? What if education was not about competition, but about contribution—not about acquiring more, but about becoming more?

For karma does not revere knowledge, but the wisdom to embody its truth. It does not reward mere accumulation, but the radiance of illumination—the light of understanding turned into action. It does not measure our worth by what we possess, but by what we pour into the world—by the love we have sown, the lives we have uplifted, and the legacy of service that echoes long after we are gone.

And when we awaken from the illusion of separateness—when we cast aside the falsehood that we are solitary beings struggling against the tides of life—we come to know the highest truth:

We are not here to control, but to create. Not to ascend above others, but to rise with them. Not to grasp, but to give—to serve, to uplift, to become the beacon that guides others toward their own light.

To truly understand karma is to walk the sacred path of service—to recognize that every action, every thought, every offering ripples far beyond what we can see. It is to add the highest value—not just to our work, but to the very essence of our existence, to every breath we take, to every moment we inhabit, to every soul we encounter. For in the end, we are not mere witnesses to transformation—we are the very force through which it unfolds.

Chapter 11

Adding the Highest Value

Deep within each of us lies a quiet yet insatiable longing—a yearning not just to exist, but to create, to shape, to merge our inner world with the outer. It is an ancient force, woven into the very fabric of our being, calling us toward something greater than mere survival. It is the pull of purpose, the whisper of destiny urging us to leave an imprint upon the world.

But fulfillment does not come from mere action—it emerges from the profound discovery of what makes us truly unique. Before we can add the highest value to the world, we must first ask: "What is my uniqueness? What am I naturally gifted at?" It is in this revelation that mastery begins, for only when we uncover and refine our inherent strengths can we channel them toward something far greater than ourselves.

The wisdom of adding the highest value is deep, but it is incomplete without self-discovery. Giving is not just about generosity—it is about excellence. It is about honing that singular gift that no one else can offer in quite the same way. Our greatest impact does not come from simply working hard or serving blindly; it comes from unlocking the rare, irreplaceable essence within us. When we recognize our natural inclinations, develop them with unwavering dedication, and share them with intention, we are no longer just adding value—we are adding the highest value.

The Search for Uniqueness

Our life's purpose, though elusive to many, becomes undeniable when we embrace the question: "What is my uniqueness?" It is not something to be created or manufactured—it is something to be discovered. It is not found in comparison, but in recognition.

Every soul is born with a distinct composition of strengths, perspectives, and passions. Some find their brilliance in artistry or innovation, others in leadership, teaching, or problem-solving. And yet, so often, we drift through life without ever pausing to reflect:

"What comes effortlessly to me that others find difficult?"
"What fills me with energy and purpose?"
"What makes me lose track of time, where my mind and heart are in complete harmony?"

These questions are not just musings; they are keys that unlock the gateway to mastery. When we stop chasing external validation and begin listening to the silent wisdom within, a new path emerges. No longer do we operate from mere obligation or survival; instead, we step into a higher realm—not abstract or distant, but tangible and real. We begin to engage with life in a way that elevates every interaction, every creation, and every endeavor.

Mastery is not about being the best at everything—it is about being exceptional in something. It is about dedicating ourselves to refinement, to lifelong learning, to becoming so skilled in our area of excellence that our presence leaves an indelible mark. When we move with this awareness, success is no longer something we chase— it becomes something we embody.

The Universal Psychology of Mastery and Contribution

To grasp the essence of adding the highest value, we need only turn to the wisdom of nature—the silent teacher that, since the dawn of time, has orchestrated the symphony of existence with effortless harmony. In nature, there is no resistance, no striving for validation, no need to prove worth. Every element simply is, fulfilling its purpose with quiet precision, adding value not through force but through alignment with its intrinsic design.

Consider an apple tree. It does not waste its energy yearning to be a rosebush, nor does it envy the height of the oak that stands beside it. It does not hesitate, compare, or seek approval. Instead, it simply grows, absorbing the warmth of the sun, drawing nourishment from the earth, and fulfilling its purpose with quiet grace—producing fruit, season after season, because that is what it was created to do. And in doing so, it nourishes the world, offering its bounty freely, without hesitation or demand.

The river, too, does not resist its nature. It does not lament that it is not the sky, nor does it seek to control the course it must take. It moves with effortless certainty, carving through rock, shaping the land, offering life to all who depend upon its flow. The sun does not withhold its light until it is asked to shine, nor does the eagle second-guess its ability to soar. Each thrives, not because it competes or conforms, but because it embraces its own essence, existing in perfect alignment with the purpose it was meant to fulfill.

And so it must be with us. We were not meant to walk a path dictated by expectation or shaped by the molds of conformity. We were not designed to suppress our gifts in pursuit of someone else's definition of success. Like the tree, the river, and the stars, we are meant to thrive in the spaces where our natural abilities shine, where our gifts—once discovered, cultivated, and refined—flow outward in service to something greater than ourselves.

When we fully embrace the idea that we serve the Universal Power best by excelling in what we are naturally gifted at, everything shifts. Success is no longer measured by external achievement—it becomes an act of devotion, an honoring of the divine potential placed within us. Adding the highest value is no longer a task to be completed or a burden to be carried; it becomes a way of being—an eternal unfolding, where each day invites us to refine our skill, elevate our creativity, and deepen our impact.

A Real-World Practice of Adding the Highest Value

Allow me to share a real example of this principle in action—a defining moment from my time leading POLY-CARB, where the philosophy of adding the highest value shaped not just a business decision, but a legacy.

In the early 1980s, POLY-CARB's product, FLEXOGRID, was selected for a bridge project in Chillicothe, Ohio. FLEXOGRID, a revolutionary waterproof overlay, was designed to protect bridge decks from the corrosive effects of road salt, prolonging their life and ensuring greater safety for drivers. However, due to improper application by the contractor, the final result did not meet our standards. Though POLY-CARB bore no fault in the outcome, and we had been fully paid, we faced a choice: either accept the completed work as it was, adhering to standard business practices, or take the road less traveled.

Conventional business logic would have dictated that we walk away. But POLY-CARB's foundation was built on a deeper philosophy—the principle of adding the highest value. To simply accept mediocrity, even when justified, was not in alignment with our purpose.

We made the decision to redo the entire project at our own cost—a staggering $250,000 investment that wiped out any potential profit. State engineers were bewildered. "No one has asked you to redo this," they said. "There's no regulatory requirement." But to us, the real measure of success was not financial—it was integrity.

What followed was beyond what we had envisioned. The decision to uphold our highest standard—without obligation or expectation—created ripples far beyond a single project. Our methods and findings gained national recognition, our product became an industry benchmark, and our unwavering commitment to excellence established POLY-CARB as a name synonymous with integrity.

This experience revealed a profound truth: when we commit to adding the highest value, we attract rewards that far exceed financial gain. Service, when offered from a place of true mastery and integrity, reshapes not only the world around us but the very fabric of who we are.

Integrating the Concept into Education

To weave the principle of adding the highest value into the fabric of education, we must dismantle the old paradigms that confine learning to mere accumulation—of facts memorized, exams conquered, degrees obtained. Education must transcend this rigid framework. It must cease to be a system of external achievement and become what it was always meant to be—a sacred journey of self-discovery. A voyage not toward a predetermined destination, but toward the revelation of one's singular essence.

It must guide students not to ask, How can I succeed? but rather: "What is my natural gift?" "What am I uniquely capable of mastering?" "How can I refine this gift to create the greatest impact?"

This shift redefines education—not as a race for validation but as an awakening. It releases students from the narrow corridors of competition and ushers them into the vast expanse of self-realization. No longer do they seek approval; they seek purpose. No longer do they pursue mere accomplishments; they pursue mastery—the mastery of the rare, irreplaceable essence within them.

When this awareness takes root, every action—however small— becomes an offering. Every lesson, every endeavor is infused with meaning, not for the sake of applause, but for the sheer joy of refinement. In this light, learning is no longer a means to an end; it is an act of devotion, an eternal dialogue between one's potential and its highest expression.

In the grand design of existence, each of us carries a singular thread—an offering only we can weave into the vast and intricate tapestry of the world. No two threads are alike; no two expressions are identical. The greatest value we can add does not lie in imitation, nor in retracing the steps of others. It is found in the unearthing of our own essence, our own brilliance, and in the fearless embodiment of who we were always meant to be.

It is in authenticity, not replication, that our true power is revealed. It is in the bold pursuit of our innate gifts—the talents and inclinations so deeply woven into our being that they feel less like acquired skills and more like echoes of something eternal. To add the highest value is not to conform to expectation, but to unearth the rarest, deepest truth within us and give it form—to let it breathe, to let it shine, brilliant, unshaken, and whole.

This journey is not about external validation. It is not about the fleeting markers of success—titles, wealth, prestige. True fulfillment is born of mastery—not mastery for the sake of dominance, but mastery as a sacred act of service.

Mastery is a covenant between self and soul. It is a lifelong refinement of what we alone can bring into existence. It is a sculptor's devotion, chiseling away the unnecessary until only the essence remains. It is the dancer's surrender, the writer's ink, the thinker's revelation—a process of endless becoming, where each breakthrough is not an arrival but an invitation to go further still.

When we nurture our uniqueness with dedication, discipline, and an unwavering commitment to growth, we do more than succeed—we serve. We become vessels for something greater than ourselves, conduits through which the Universal Power of Oneness flows freely. We no longer strive merely to fit into the world; we rise to elevate it.

For in the end, adding the highest value is not a mere milestone, not a prize to be claimed or a goal to be reached—it is an eternal unfolding. A continuous evolution. A journey without end, where every step forward is both a destination and a new beginning.

And when education is built upon this foundation—when learning is no longer about fitting into the world but about transforming it—we will no longer produce mere professionals. We will cultivate visionaries. We will raise thinkers, creators, and innovators who do not measure success by what they acquire but by what they offer.

They will be the architects of a new world—one where every thread is woven with purpose, where the tapestry of humanity is made ever richer, ever more luminous, by those who dare to discover, refine, and share their highest gifts.

This, indeed, is the path of the lifelong learner—the seeker—the creator—the keeper of truth. It is the path of those who understand that education is not a means to an end, but a lifelong pilgrimage into the infinite expanse of wisdom, self-mastery, and service to the greater whole.

Chapter 12

Becoming the Ultimate Lifelong Learner

From the earliest whispers of my childhood, my mother bestowed upon me two guiding stars, luminous beacons that would shape my understanding of both triumph and tranquility: to embrace an unwavering, unconditional gratitude, no matter the storm that life may summon, and to forever seek the refinement of one's best to make it better. These words, imbued with a quiet grandeur, seemed beautiful yet distant in my youth. It would take years for their depths to unfurl before me, like petals yielding to the dawn.

Gratitude without condition perplexed me for much of my life. I had always believed that gratitude required a catalyst—a reason, a gift, a moment of serendipity. Are we not taught to be thankful for our fortunes, to chronicle blessings in journals, to bow our heads before meals in reverence? How, then, could gratitude exist independent of circumstance? This question lingered like an echo in the corridors of my mind, until an unexpected revelation emerged through my daughter, Nisha, illuminating what I had yet to understand.

One morning, as I drove Nisha to school, a question leapt from my lips, carrying with it an unforeseen lesson. "If God stood before you and granted you a single wish—anything your heart desired— what would you ask for?" Her wide eyes sparkled with contemplation before she ventured, "Could I ask for unlimited money?"—the innocent reply of a child imagining the boundless wonders such a wish could bring. I assured her that such a request was certainly possible.

Yet, as we unraveled the consequences of each grand desire, she began to discern their veiled burdens. An endless fortune, she mused, would dull the thrill of a hard-earned victory, would strip surprise from generosity. Immortality, she reasoned, might render life a monotonous waltz, its brevity the very thing that lent it meaning. Even fame, she foresaw, could erode the quiet joys of freedom and privacy. Each wish, we realized, bore a shadow, an unforeseen cost.

Then, after a moment of reflection, she turned to me and asked, "Dad, is there something wrong with me if I don't want anything from God? What if I'm just grateful for what He's already given me?" Her words, simple yet profound, settled upon me like a revelation. In that moment, my daughter became my teacher. True gratitude, I understood then, does not tether itself to acquisition or circumstance. It is not an occasional visitor but a steady companion, a way of being rather than a fleeting emotion.

The Power of Lifelong Learning

The second principle my mother imparted to me—the relentless pursuit of making one's best even better—required time to reveal its true essence. It lingered in my mind like an unsolved riddle, waiting for the wisdom of experience to unlock its meaning. How could the pinnacle of my ability still demand refinement? If something is my 'best,' how could it be surpassed? The answer did not arrive in words but in the quiet revelation of life itself—woven into the living poetry of my wife, Dolly.

Dolly moves through the world with the grace of an artist and the devotion of a saint, transforming the mundane into the extraordinary. She does not merely complete tasks—she elevates them, imbuing every gesture with care, every effort with reverence. The simple act of arranging flowers becomes an offering, the preparation of a meal an expression of love, the smallest kindness a masterpiece of intention. In her presence, I witnessed an unspoken truth: excellence is not a fixed point but an ever-unfolding horizon, always calling us forward.

Through Dolly, I came to understand that refinement is not about perfection, nor is it about outpacing oneself in an endless race of achievement. Rather, it is about deepening the artistry of our existence, expanding the capacity of our hearts, and sharpening the instruments of our purpose. Growth, I realized, is not a burden but a gift—an invitation to participate in the great unfolding of our potential.

And this ceaseless striving is not fueled by ambition alone; it is a higher form of service. To evolve, to expand, to learn without end is not merely an act of self-improvement but a tribute to the divine intelligence that breathes life into our being. It is to recognize that the talents we have been given are not possessions, but responsibilities. That every skill we refine, every lesson we absorb, every mastery we pursue is not meant for our benefit alone but for the elevation of those around us.

To commit to lifelong learning is to step into harmony with the rhythm of the universe, which knows no stagnation, no final arrival. The river does not question why it must keep flowing; the tree does not resist the call to stretch toward the heavens. So too must we embrace our own evolution—not as a means of conquest, but as a sacred duty, an offering of gratitude for the gift of existence itself.

For in the end, to learn endlessly is to love endlessly—to love life, to love wisdom, and to love the infinite possibility within ourselves and each other.

Cultivating Wisdom in Education

Imagine if these sacred principles—gratitude, lifelong learning, and self-betterment—were woven into the very tapestry of education. If, from their earliest days, children were guided to view learning not as a stepping stone to personal success but as a path to discovering and fulfilling their highest calling in service to the world, then the classroom itself would transform into a place of profound growth.

A practice of daily gratitude would anchor students in the present, fostering a perspective that sees blessings in even the smallest moments. Rather than gratitude being reserved for special occasions, it would become a daily ritual, instilling in them the same awareness Nisha displayed—a sense that gratitude is a state of being, not contingent upon possessions or achievements. Through stories and reflections like Nisha's, students would learn that gratitude does not depend on external circumstances, helping them find joy in life's everyday wonders.

The concept of making one's best better would revolutionize the learning experience. Instead of focusing solely on grades, students would be encouraged to approach each assignment as an opportunity for self-discovery and continuous improvement. They would see success not as an endpoint but as an evolving process, where growth is valued over perfection. Imagine art projects, science experiments, and creative writing assignments where the goal is not merely to do well but to ask, "How can I grow in this? How can I make my best better?"

And in this reimagined classroom, collaboration would not be a contest of individual prowess but a collective endeavor. The notion of competition would be replaced with one of interdependence—students learning not to outshine but to uplift, to ask not "How can I stand above?" but "How can I help us rise together?" This is the ethos of interconnectedness, a recognition that our truest fulfillment lies not in solitary victories but in shared ascension.

A Paradigm Shift in Education

For generations, traditional education has mirrored the limitations of the human body mindset—a paradigm rooted in competition, self-driven ambition, and survival instinct, governed by the question: "What's in it for me?" In this framework, learning becomes transactional, pursued not for the expansion of consciousness but as a means to an end—to affirm identity, accumulate status, and secure a sense of control. Success is measured by external validation, and knowledge is hoarded as a possession rather than shared as a force for illumination.

Yet, when we shift from this fragmented perspective to one of interconnectedness, education transcends its conventional role. It ceases to be a mere tool for individual advancement and instead becomes a sacred bridge—one that leads not only to self-discovery but to service. In this expansive vision, learning is no longer confined to personal ambition; it becomes an unfolding of purpose, a way to harness one's unique gifts and talents in service to the greater whole. Knowledge is no longer a commodity—it is a light, illuminating not just our own path, but the paths of those around us.

By weaving together the threads of unconditional gratitude and the eternal pursuit of self-improvement, education would cease to be merely an institution—it would become a pilgrimage of self-realization. Students would not merely prepare for a future profession; they would prepare to shape the world with wisdom, compassion, and an unyielding commitment to growth.

Gratitude would be the foundation, lifelong learning the journey, and the refinement of one's best the compass that guides the way. Students would not simply be equipped to survive in an ever-changing world; they would be empowered to thrive, to adapt, to create, and most importantly, to serve.

In this new paradigm, education is not the filling of a vessel but the kindling of a fire—a flame that burns with curiosity, humility, and an insatiable desire to make every moment, every lesson, every endeavor a step toward something greater. And in doing so, education does not merely prepare young minds for the world; it inspires them to transform it.

This is the heart of lifelong learning—not just as an academic pursuit, but as a way of life on the path to self-alignment. It is the endless dance between gratitude and growth, the delicate balance between acceptance and ambition. It is the realization that learning does not conclude with a diploma but is, in fact, the very rhythm of an awakened life. And when we embrace this truth, we are no longer just students in a classroom—we become students of the universe itself.

Chapter 13

Self-Alignment: Integrating Holistic Practices into Our Lives and Education

In the quiet spaces where the mind meets the soul, a radiant path begins to unfold—the journey of self-alignment. First whispered by Eastern sages and now gently embraced by a Western world long entangled in the machinery of modernity, this path is more than a method; it is a poetic reclamation of balance, purpose, and a deep, abiding fulfillment that transcends the endless chase for productivity.

In an age when success is often measured by relentless outputs and transient achievements, the yearning for inner harmony grows ever more urgent. It calls upon us to rediscover the art of living with mindful grace and to weave a tapestry of holistic practices that nurture our body, mind, and spirit in equal measure.

The Emergence of a New Consciousness

For centuries, the Western spirit was ensnared in a mechanistic waltz with progress—a worldview in which the body was seen merely as a vessel for ambition and fleeting gratification. But as the pressures of modern life began to unravel the fabric of our collective well-being, a quiet revolution stirred beneath the surface.

In the transformative counterculture of the 1960s, hearts and minds began to awaken to the whisper of a deeper purpose. The winds of change carried new questions—about meaning, about wholeness, about the forgotten sanctity of life.

Today, self-alignment is echoed in whispered mantras and illuminated gatherings, in books that invite us inward, and in classes that offer glimpses of a more soulful way to live. Yet many still skim the surface—touching serenity in fleeting moments, but never fully immersing in the deeper waters of transformation. Commercialization has often diluted these ancient teachings, reducing them to checklists or spiritual décor. But true self-alignment—like a sacred garden—cannot be rushed. It must be nurtured daily, tended with care, intention, and reverence. It is a lifelong devotion to the harmonious weaving of body, mind, and spirit into a unified, vibrant whole.

Two Essential Mindsets: The Veil and the Vision

At the heart of self-alignment lies a profound choice between two distinct ways of perceiving our existence. The first mindset, which we may call the Veil, sees the body as a transient vessel—an instrument merely for satisfying fleeting desires and immediate needs. In this view, life is a series of quick fixes, where every pleasure is temporary and every achievement is soon eclipsed by the next challenge. Driven by insecurity and the ever-whispering voice of the illusory self, this mindset ensnares us in a cycle of indulgence and regret, leaving us perpetually yearning for more.

In stark contrast stands the Vision—a perspective that honors the body as a sacred temple, a resplendent vessel imbued with the essence of Universal Power. With this elevated vision, every act of self-care becomes a deliberate ritual of reverence, an opportunity to commune with the divine pulse that animates our very being. When we see ourselves through this lens, our habits transform into acts of love and devotion; every mindful breath, every conscious choice, is a step toward harmonizing our inner and outer worlds. This is the pathway to lasting well-being—a journey where the pursuit of pleasure is replaced by the quest for profound, enduring fulfillment.

Self-Alignment in Education: Instilling Lifelong Practices Early

Imagine an educational landscape where the principles of self-alignment are woven into the very fabric of daily life—a place where the pursuit of knowledge is inseparable from the cultivation of inner balance. In such a world, schools transform into sanctuaries of the soul, nurturing not only academic achievement but also the sacred art of living mindfully.

In this visionary approach, the classroom becomes a microcosm of holistic well-being. Students are introduced early to practices that honor the body as a temple and the mind as a boundless reservoir of potential. Through gentle rituals of self-care and mindfulness, young learners come to understand that true success is measured not by the rapid accumulation of accolades, but by the quiet strength of inner resilience and the harmony of spirit. With every lesson, they discover that nurturing their inner world is as essential as mastering any academic subject—a lifelong gift that prepares them to navigate the complexities of life with grace and purpose.

Step 1: Daily Cleansing as an Act of Sacred Renewal

At the foundation of self-alignment lies the ritual of daily cleansing— a practice that transcends mere physical hygiene to become an act of profound self-respect. In every drop of water, there is a whisper of life's ancient essence, a reminder that renewal is both natural and sacred. To drink water is to invite clarity into every cell, to wash away the residues of fatigue and tension, and to honor the body as the vessel of our deepest potential.

This ritual of hydration supports our well-being on multiple levels, nurturing both the physical and the mental. Water's vital presence aids digestion, supports circulation, and optimizes the function of key organs such as the liver and kidneys, which in turn enhances our mental clarity and overall physical health. When schools weave this practice into their daily routines, they create a living curriculum of wellness.

Health education programs can illuminate the myriad benefits of hydration—not just as a means to sustain life but as an essential pillar of cognitive focus, mood stability, and robust health. Imagine a classroom where dedicated water breaks and the inclusion of water-rich foods like fruits and vegetables become celebrated rituals, each sip and each bite a step toward holistic well-being. In embracing these practices, students learn early that caring for the body is an act of reverence, a gentle acknowledgment of the interwoven nature of body, mind, and spirit—a lifelong commitment to honoring the temple of life within.

Step 2: External Cleansing

Just as our inner selves flourish in the light of clarity and order, our external surroundings yearn for mindful care—a reverent touch that transforms everyday environments into sanctuaries of beauty and peace. External cleansing is more than a chore; it is an act of homage to the spaces we inhabit. The timeless adage "Cleanliness is next to Godliness" resonates deeply here, reminding us that by treating our environments as sacred extensions of ourselves, we nurture our mental, emotional, and spiritual well-being.

Daily bathing emerges as a profound ritual that goes far beyond mere physical refreshment. It is a ceremonial immersion in the present moment—a practice where the warm embrace of water washes away not only physical impurities but also the residue of old worries, unhealed emotions, and burdens of the past. In this quiet ritual, we find an opportunity to shed old patterns and to renew our commitment to self-care. Each bath, each cleansing, becomes a symbolic act of letting go, a metaphorical purging that frees us to reconnect with our truest selves and to step forward with renewed vitality and grace.

Yet external cleansing extends its reach beyond our personal rituals to the spaces that shape our daily lives—our homes, classrooms, workplaces, and even the vehicles that carry us through our journeys. These spaces, when cluttered or neglected, can weigh upon our psyche, breeding disorganization and a sense of disquiet. By consciously tending to our surroundings, we create environments that mirror the order and serenity we seek within ourselves. Regular tidying and organizing transform spaces into harmonious sanctuaries where creativity, productivity, and calm can thrive. In doing so, we not only uplift our own spirits but also foster an atmosphere of respect and compassion that benefits everyone who shares these spaces with us. Through the art of external cleansing, we embrace a daily practice of self-respect and communal care—an invitation to cultivate beauty, balance, and a profound sense of well-being in every corner of our lives.

Step 3: Daily Fresh Air and Breathing for Mental Clarity

There is a delicate poetry in the act of breathing—a rhythmic dance between our inner world and the vast expanse of the cosmos. Each inhalation draws in the life-affirming essence of nature, while every exhalation releases the weight of our worries into the open sky. In these moments, we rediscover the simple yet profound truth that every breath is an invitation to reconnect with our innermost self.

Fresh air and breathing exercises help maintain the vitality of our inner temple. Implementing short breathing exercises in classrooms not only aids focus but also helps students connect with their breath as a calming tool. Techniques such as deep breathing or alternate nostril breathing could be introduced as brief "mindful moments" throughout the school day, helping students discover the power of breath for calming and centering the mind. These mindful breaths not only enhance concentration and clarity but also serve as gentle reminders of our connection to the natural world—a world that is as essential to our well-being as the air we breathe.

Step 4: Strength and Flexibility as Tools for Lifelong Health

The body, in all its intricate beauty, is a dynamic interplay of strength and flexibility—a living expression of resilience and grace. Practices such as yoga epitomize this delicate balance, transforming physical movement into a poetic dance that unites body and spirit. In the fluid motion of each pose, the body learns to express its innate wisdom, cultivating both physical endurance and inner calm.

Introducing such practices into the realm of education redefines physical education as more than mere sport—it becomes a celebration of life's harmonious rhythms. Through yoga and other mindful exercises, students learn to honor their bodies as sanctuaries of potential and expression. They discover that true strength is not measured solely by muscle or might, but by the capacity to move with both purpose and gentleness, navigating life's challenges with a balanced heart and a flexible spirit.

Step 5: Nutrition Education to Sustain the Body as a Sacred Vessel

Food, in all its vibrant diversity, is the tangible expression of nature's abundance—a sacred offering that nourishes our body and sustains our spirit. When approached with mindfulness, every meal becomes a ritual of gratitude, an opportunity to honor the intricate connection between what we consume and the vitality it imparts.

In an educational setting, lessons on nutrition transcend the mechanics of diet and calorie counting; they become an exploration of the alchemical relationship between food and life. Students are invited to see each ingredient as a vital component of a grand symphony—a mosaic of colors, textures, and flavors that not only sustains the body but also enriches the soul. Through mindful eating practices and thoughtful reflection on the origins of their food, young learners come to appreciate that nourishment is not a mere physical need but a profound, sacred dialogue with nature itself.

Fostering Inner Alignment Through Spiritual Awareness

Beyond the realm of physical practices lies the expansive journey of inner awakening—a quest to rediscover our place within the vast tapestry of existence. Fostering inner alignment invites us to explore the deeper dimensions of spirituality, to engage with the timeless wisdom of diverse traditions, and to recognize that our individual well-being is inextricably linked to the collective pulse of the universe.

In this space of contemplative inquiry, ancient teachings and modern insights converge, guiding us toward a vision of life where every moment is infused with purpose and every experience is a step on the path to self-realization. Educational explorations into world philosophies, meditative practices, and mystical traditions empower students to question, reflect, and ultimately connect with the inner light that guides us all. Here, the journey of self-alignment becomes not only a personal odyssey but a shared voyage—a collective awakening to the truth that we are all part of a vast, interconnected whole.

Infusing Self-Alignment into Daily Learning

When self-alignment is embraced as a core principle of education, the act of learning is transformed into a soulful pilgrimage—a journey where academic pursuits are interwoven with the practices of mindfulness and self-care. In such an enriched environment, every lesson is imbued with the gentle wisdom of introspection, every challenge reframed as an opportunity to cultivate inner strength, and every success celebrated not only as an external achievement but as a harmonious convergence of heart and mind.

In classrooms where self-alignment is nurtured, teachers become both mentors and guides—illuminating paths of discovery that honor the whole person. Students learn that true education extends far beyond textbooks and examinations; it is a lifelong process of growth, reflection, and soulful connection. Beginning from a young age, they build habits that not only ensure lifelong health but cultivate an enduring connection to themselves and the world. They realize that life's highest aim is not simply achievement but alignment, service, and unity with all around them.

Chapter 14

The Re-Alignment Habits

As we explored in Chapter 4, our habits shape every facet of our lives. They are the quiet architects of our daily existence—gifts that allow our minds and bodies to operate on a gentle, rhythmic autopilot. In their silent efficiency, they guide us through the labyrinth of life, sparing us the weariness of endless deliberation and bestowing upon us a sense of freedom and ease.

Yet, as with all potent forces, the power of habits is double-edged. They can be the bright lanterns illuminating our paths to growth, or they can become the chains that bind us to familiar yet stifling patterns. In the tender years of childhood, the seeds of habit are sown deep, laying the groundwork for future triumphs or trials. Whether through our choices in nourishment, our commitment to exercise, our mental focus, or our pursuit of lifelong learning, the early cultivation of constructive habits heralds an ascent toward a life replete with fulfillment and enduring success.

Good habits are not confined to the classroom or the pages of textbooks. They permeate every dimension of life, forming the backbone of a holistic self-development. A transformative education transcends the accumulation of knowledge—it is the art of weaving habits that resonate with universal truths. When these habits are steeped in service, integrity, and the timeless inquiry, "What am I here to give?" they blossom into tools of self-discovery and pillars of societal contribution.

Habits: Our Greatest Strength or Weakness

Much of what we dismiss as "bad habits" often germinates in the soil of insecurity, fear, greed, stress, or the unchallenged conditioning of society. They are the quiet whispers of external influences—family, culture, religion, or environment—that slowly inscribe limitations upon our souls. Unchecked, these habits become the crutches that confine our potential, chaining us to cycles of dissatisfaction and self-doubt, where reaction replaces intention and life's vibrant canvas fades into monotony.

In contrast, habits nurtured in the light of self-alignment—those that echo the universal wisdom and a heartfelt commitment to serve— unlock the portals to sustainable success and inner tranquility. These are the habits that liberate us from the relentless pursuit of external accolades and anchor us in a purpose-filled existence, where every moment becomes a celebration of empowerment and joy.

Traditional wisdom counsels that to break a habit, one must replace it with a positive alternative, avoid familiar triggers, and seek out nurturing environments. Yet a deeper metamorphosis unfolds when we shift our perspective entirely—when we forsake the clamor of outer persona and attune ourselves to the silent rhythm of universal truth.

This re-alignment calls for habits that weave us into the grand tapestry of life. Habits grounded in service, gratitude, and an unyielding commitment to self-improvement become the very bedrock of our daily actions. They guide us to transcend the ephemeral allure of external validation and root us in the fertile soil of purpose, crafting a life rich in meaning and interconnectedness.

The 12 Self-Integration Habits

These twelve sacred practices form an empowering framework for re-alignment—a pathway to break free from limiting patterns and embrace a life of intentional growth and heartfelt contribution:

1. **Gratitude as a Way of Life:** Imagine waking each morning to the quiet murmur of your heart, listing the blessings—both grand and subtle—that adorn your life. Gratitude is more than a fleeting thank-you; it is a deep, soulful recognition of life's

intricate tapestry. In every challenge, there is a hidden lesson, a seed of growth waiting to bloom. By embracing gratitude unconditionally, we shift our vision from what is missing to the abundant beauty that surrounds us, transforming trials into triumphs and imbuing our days with creative energy and resilient hope.

2. **Living in Self-Alignment:** At its core, self-alignment is the art of tuning your inner compass to the rhythm of the universe. It is recognizing that every action, thought, and emotion is intertwined with a greater whole. When we live in self-alignment, we embrace our role as part of a vast, interconnected mosaic, where each gesture of kindness, every act of service, reinforces the integrity of our shared existence. This habit calls us to walk our path with authenticity, honor, and a deep respect for the bonds that unite us all.

3. **Embracing an Abundance Mentality:** To embrace abundance is to cast aside the shadows of scarcity and fear, and to see the universe as an endless wellspring of possibilities. This mindset nurtures a spirit of generosity, where one's successes are not measured by personal gain but by the positive impact radiated outward. With each act of giving, we create ripples that transform our communities and affirm the belief that there is more than enough to nourish every dream, every aspiration, and every heart. Liberate yourself from the confines of scarcity. Know that the universe offers bountiful resources for those who channel them to elevate others.

4. **Practicing Frugality with Purpose:** Frugality, when embraced with mindful intention, transcends mere thriftiness. It becomes an art form—an elegant dance of resourcefulness that honors every material gift as a stepping stone toward excellence. This habit teaches us to steward our resources with wisdom, to invest in quality over quantity, and to view every expenditure as an opportunity to build a more sustainable and meaningful future for ourselves and those around us.

5. **Remaining in Student Mode:** Life is an eternal classroom where every moment is a lesson. Embracing the perpetual role of a student means nurturing an insatiable curiosity and a willingness to learn from every experience—be it a success or a setback. This habit invites us to approach life with humility, to ask questions fearlessly, and to see the world as a vast repository of wisdom waiting to be discovered. It is through this endless quest for knowledge that we continually evolve and refine our understanding of ourselves and the world.

6. **Pursuing Excellence with the Spirit of Perfection: Making Our Best Better:** Perfection, when seen as an absolute, can become a harsh and unattainable illusion—but when embraced as a spirit, it becomes a sacred compass that gently urges us toward the continual refinement of our gifts. To pursue excellence with the spirit of perfection is to engage in the daily devotion of growth—not for validation or applause, but out of reverence for the potential that resides within us. This habit is about making our best better, moment by moment, not by chasing flawlessness, but by honoring the process of becoming. It invites us to rise above comparison, to approach each step with humility, and to transform effort into impact through conscious intention. In this practice, we are freed from the tyranny of unrealistic standards and guided instead by the joy of purposeful progress. Excellence, fueled by the essence of perfection, becomes not an endpoint, but a lifelong path—a way of living with integrity, mastery, and the quiet courage to evolve.

7. **Fostering Discipline and Intensity:** Discipline is the steady drumbeat that propels us forward, while intensity is the flame that ignites our passions. Together, they create a powerful synergy that transforms intention into action. By cultivating a disciplined approach—marked by focus, determination, and unwavering commitment—we channel

our energy into meaningful pursuits. This habit teaches us to prioritize with clarity, to work diligently towards our goals, and to infuse every endeavor with a deep, purposeful vigor. Honor the sanctity of time with focus and dedication, turning disciplined effort into the fertile ground from which true mastery blooms.

8. **Finishing What You Start:** There is a quiet power in completion—a sense of fulfillment that arises when we see our projects through to their natural end. Finishing what we start is more than a habit of productivity; it is a testament to our integrity and resolve. It requires us to confront procrastination, to overcome self-doubt, and to commit wholeheartedly to our chosen paths. Each completed task builds momentum, fostering confidence and reinforcing the belief that every endeavor, no matter how challenging, is a step toward a more accomplished self. Cast off the allure of procrastination. Commit fully to your pursuits, building momentum and a deep, resonant sense of accomplishment.

9. **Living with Enthusiasm:** Enthusiasm is the glowing spark that transforms everyday activities into vibrant celebrations of life. It is an energy that fuels creativity, motivates perseverance, and infuses our actions with joy. When we live with enthusiasm, we greet challenges with a smile, viewing them as opportunities to learn and grow. This habit inspires those around us, creating a contagious atmosphere where passion and positivity become the cornerstones of every experience. Let enthusiasm be the vibrant flame that transforms obstacles into stepping stones and labor into a dance of joy.

10. **Operating in the Present:** The present moment is a sanctuary—a fleeting yet infinite space where true creativity and excellence reside. Operating in the present calls us to let go of the regrets of the past and the anxieties of the future, to immerse ourselves fully in the here and now. It is in this sacred moment that our actions are most potent, our

decisions most authentic, and our connection to life most profound. By anchoring ourselves in the present, we harness the transformative power of now and discover the limitless possibilities that emerge when we live fully in each breath. Release the ghosts of past regrets and future anxieties; immerse yourself wholly in the rich, fertile soil of the present moment.

11. **Practicing Unconditional Living:** Unconditional living is the brave act of embracing life without reservations or predetermined expectations. It is a habit of openness—a willingness to accept and act upon life's offerings, irrespective of external conditions. This approach liberates us from the confines of societal norms and self-imposed limitations, allowing us to respond to life with authenticity, spontaneity, and an unfettered heart. In practicing unconditional living, we learn to love, serve, and engage with the world in its raw, unfiltered beauty. Abandon the chains of conditional expectations. Embrace life with open arms, ready to act with spontaneity and grace.

12. **Keeping a Clear Purpose in Mind:** A clear purpose is the North Star that guides our every action—a celestial beacon that reminds us of our higher calling. Anchoring each deed in the question, "How can I serve and add the highest value?" transforms routine tasks into meaningful contributions. This habit infuses our lives with clarity and direction, aligning our daily choices with our deepest values and aspirations. It is a continual reminder that every moment is an opportunity to leave an indelible mark on the world, building a legacy of service, compassion, and boundless impact.

A Life of Conscious Practice

Habits are not mere routines; they are the very architecture of our character, the silent verses in the poetry of our lives. When harmonized with universal truths, they transform into a living testament to our innermost values and aspirations. Each habit, like a delicate brushstroke on a vast canvas, contributes to the masterpiece of a life consciously crafted—transcending the mundane to embrace a realm of profound intentionality.

In the realm of relationships, the gentle art of gratitude transforms ordinary interactions into symphonies of empathy and understanding. A steadfast commitment to self-alignment lays the foundation for trust and integrity, while an abundant mindset converts the competitive cacophony of life into a collaborative chorus. These practices ripple outward, touching the lives of others and weaving a tapestry of shared human experience that is as intricate as it is beautiful.

Embedding Habits into Education

To nurture a generation that thrives in alignment, we must infuse these transformative habits into the very fabric of education. Envision classrooms where the morning light is met with moments of reflective gratitude, cultivating an ethos of abundance and possibility. Imagine a curriculum that prizes curiosity over rote memorization, encouraging young minds to explore, question, and innovate. Picture teachers as radiant beacons, inspiring their students to pursue excellence—not as an elusive perfection, but as a continuous, passionate journey of self-discovery.

Such an education transcends the boundaries of academics. It nurtures the tender shoots of emotional intelligence, fosters ethical discernment, and instills a profound sense of global responsibility. By embedding the 12 Self-Integration Habits into everyday learning, we prepare our young not merely for success, but for a life of significance—a life where each individual becomes a vital thread in the grand tapestry of humanity.

Living the Habits: Stories of Transformation

Real-life narratives often reveal what theory alone cannot—the quiet, persistent power of habits lived and breathed each day. These are not just stories, but living testaments to the alchemy that occurs when intention is transformed into consistent action.

Consider the young entrepreneur, Mehar, whose journey began in a modest city neighborhood, cradled by scarcity yet rich with kindness. With little more than determination and a heart full of gratitude, she learned early that challenges were not roadblocks, but invitations—veiled blessings calling her to rise. While others saw hardship, Mehar saw opportunity: every setback a lesson, every trial a teacher shaping the contours of a purpose-driven life.

Through savings from part-time jobs and the nurturing guidance of local mentors, Mehar dared to dream—not just of personal gain, but of creating something that could uplift many. She launched a humble venture: a café-cum-community hub that quickly became a sanctuary for local artists, thinkers, and dreamers. Each morning, before the city stirred, she sat in silence with her journal—giving thanks, setting intentions, and reaffirming her commitment to live from an abundant, generous heart. Gratitude became her compass, transforming the ordinary into the extraordinary.

Bathed in soft sunlight and the fragrance of freshly brewed coffee, her café soon evolved into something far greater than a business. It became a living, breathing community—where conversation bloomed like wildflowers, and creativity flowed freely through the cracks of shared humanity. Local painters adorned its reclaimed walls, writers found solace in steaming cups, and kindness echoed in every corner. Mehar's steadfast discipline—from sourcing the finest ingredients to the warm sincerity of her smile—cultivated an atmosphere where collaboration and creativity flourished with effortless grace.

Of course, the path was not without thorns. There were regulatory hurdles, financial tremors, and moments of aching doubt. But each time the shadows crept in, Mehar turned to her realignment habits. She returned to her journal, to stillness, to service. She revisited the clarity of her purpose—not to accumulate, but to uplift. And with each challenge, she grew—not around the storm, but through it. She was not merely surviving; she was blooming in service.

Parallel to Mehar's soulful journey is the story of John, a devoted teacher whose classroom became a sanctuary of wonder—a sacred space where curiosity unfolded like petals toward the sun. Though seasoned by years of teaching, John entered this new chapter not with certainty, but with the humility of one who knows the soul of education had been forgotten.

He had long felt that true education was more than curriculum and content—that somewhere beneath the grind of grades and metrics lay a sacred spark, waiting to be rekindled. When he discovered an approach centered on self-awareness, purpose, and inner harmony, something within him stirred to life. And so, he stepped not just into new methods, but into a new way of being.

He reimagined his classroom as a place not of instruction, but of revelation. Mornings began with stillness, not noise—five quiet minutes to invite the soul into the day. Lessons were woven like poetry, connecting numbers to nature, language to life, and knowledge to deeper knowing. Laughter was no longer a distraction but a sign of presence. Reflection was no longer an add-on, but the heartbeat of learning.

His students, once hesitant and self-conscious, began to blossom. They listened with empathy, spoke with courage, and leaned into questions rather than rushing to answers. John no longer stood above them, but beside them—not as a dispenser of facts, but as a fellow voyager on the sacred path of becoming.

At the end-of-year gathering, a mother rose to speak. Her voice was steady, but her words trembled with gratitude. "My daughter used to measure herself by grades. Now she begins her day with gratitude, reminds us to eat slowly and breathe deeply, and even made a family ritual where we each share something beautiful we noticed that day. She's learning to live, not just to achieve."

John stood in quiet awe. In that moment, he understood: to truly teach is not to fill a vessel, but to spark a flame. He had become what he was always meant to be—not just a teacher of subjects, but a cultivator of souls, a gentle craftsman of transformation.

These stories remind us that habits are not static routines, but living entities—dynamic forces that, when nurtured with intention, evolve into the very essence of our identity. They are the quiet architects of transformation, laying the foundation for lives that resonate with purpose, connection, and boundless possibility. They turn routines into rituals, tasks into offerings, and lives into legacies—not of mere survival, but of sacred contribution.

Mehar's story speaks of habits in outward action, while John's journey reveals the same habits embodied from within. Together, they illuminate that realignment is not confined to a single path—it is a universal invitation. Whether in enterprise or education, gratitude or reflection, discipline or joy, these habits become a compass guiding us back to the soul. They remind us that true change begins not with systems, but with individuals who dare to live with intention, presence, and a deep-rooted sense of purpose.

The Ultimate Unfolding of a Re-Aligned Life

In the final cadence of this exploration, we stand at the threshold of transformation—a place where the mundane dissolves into the magnificent, and every habit becomes a verse in the epic poem of existence. As the sun sets on old patterns, it rises on a new horizon of re-alignment, where each breath is a deliberate act of creation, and every step is a testament to our capacity for change.

In this luminous journey, we learn that to live in harmony with the Universe is to embrace the art of continuous self-renewal. With every moment, we have the opportunity to sculpt our destiny through habits that echo the eternal truths of gratitude, purpose, and boundless love. Let us then march forward, not with the heaviness of past failures, but with the lightness of newfound hope—each habit a stanza in our ongoing ode to life, each action a brushstroke on the ever-unfolding canvas of our soul.

And so, as this chapter closes, another unfolds—revealing that our realignment is not separate from the Universe, but an expression of its grand intelligence. The Re-Alignment Habits are not merely personal practices; they are cosmic harmonies—gateways into a greater understanding of who we are, why we are here, and how the Universe itself participates in our unfolding. In this, we are no longer merely students of habit—we become apprentices to the stars.

Chapter 15

The Psychology of the Universe

L ife unfolds as an intricate, celestial game—a grand interplay of forces both seen and unseen, where every heartbeat echoes with the wisdom of ages. To navigate this vast expanse, we must attune our inner being to the timeless rhythm of existence, discerning the dual nature of its laws: those forged by human hands, ever-shifting like desert sands, and those eternal principles that pulse at the core of the cosmos.

On one plane lie the Man-Made Laws, the constructs of our collective intellect and frailty. They mirror our evolving values, our triumphs and missteps, reflecting a society in constant flux. Yet, beyond the ephemeral confines of human design, there exists a realm of Universal Laws—immutable beacons that illuminate the path of our soul. These are the eternal truths, the unyielding principles that govern not only the mechanics of nature but also the moral and spiritual dimensions of our being.

Within this sacred domain, two distinct yet intertwined currents flow. First are the Observable Laws, the governing forces of gravity, thermodynamics, and the dance of atoms—a testament to the ordered beauty of the physical world. Then, deeper still, lie the Psychological Laws of the Universe, the subtle, ineffable edicts that shape our inner landscapes. They are the language of the cosmos, whispering secrets of morality, ethics, and the profound interconnectedness of all life.

To embrace the Psychology of the Universe is to embark on a journey toward Oneness—a state of harmonious resonance between our innermost essence and the eternal rhythms of creation. It is here that we encounter the ten luminous Universal Laws, each a shimmering thread woven into the grand tapestry of existence, like colors merging in the infinite arc of a cosmic rainbow.

1. **The Law of Integrity**

   In the vast canvas of life, no soul exists in isolation. Every act of honesty is a declaration of unity, for to wound another is to wound oneself. When we let our inner truth shine forth—uncompromised and pure—we weave bonds of trust that transcend the superficial divisions of the world. Integrity transforms every failure into fertile soil, nurturing the courage to face adversity with a clear, unburdened heart.

2. **The Law of Values**

   True values bloom from the secret garden of the soul, unfettered by the transient dictates of society. They are the silent compass that guides us through life's labyrinth, emerging naturally from our connection to the universal energy. In their gentle radiance, qualities such as honesty, empathy, and humility converge, dissolving boundaries and uniting us in the shared light of compassion.

3. **The Law of Purpose**

   Purpose is the sacred fire that kindles our passions and infuses even the most mundane tasks with cosmic significance. It calls us to dedicate each action to the greater good, transcending personal ambition to serve a collective vision. In every step we take, purpose transforms the ordinary into a ritual of creation—a continuous offering to the universal whole.

4. **The Law of Acceptance**

   Acceptance is the art of embracing the present moment in its entirety—its beauty and its challenges, its joys and its sorrows. It is the gentle surrender to life's natural flow, where every trial is a teacher and every triumph a fleeting blessing. By welcoming life without judgment, we cultivate an inner sanctuary of peace, turning adversity into the very soil from which our growth springs forth.

5. **The Law of Abundance**
    Abundance is not a scarce commodity, but a boundless, ever-flowing river that springs forth when the voice of the divided mind is silenced. It is the realization that the universe is an infinite garden, where every act of generosity and gratitude nourishes the collective harvest. In embracing this limitless bounty, we dispel fear and envy, replacing them with the celestial joy of giving and the serene pleasure of receiving.

6. **The Law of Leadership**
    True leadership arises from the mastery of oneself—a radiant beacon that guides others through the murkiness of uncertainty. It is not the exercise of power over others, but the gentle art of inspiring and uniting hearts through wisdom, empathy, and service. A leader who walks this path emanates authenticity, setting in motion a ripple of transformation that elevates all who follow.

7. **The Law of Freedom**
    Freedom, in its most profound sense, is the liberation of the soul—a state of being achieved not by discarding discipline, but by aligning with a higher, purposeful order. It is the exquisite balance between structure and spontaneity, where every disciplined act becomes a stepping stone to creative liberation. In this harmonious dance, we find clarity and serenity, soaring beyond the confines of self-imposed limitations.

8. **The Law of Change**
    Change is the eternal pulse that animates the universe—a ceaseless, rhythmic evolution that shapes our destiny. Every ending heralds a new beginning, every setback conceals the seed of future triumph. Embracing change is to dance with time itself, flowing gracefully with the currents of

transformation and welcoming each new chapter as an invitation to grow.

9. **The Law of Grace**

Grace is the tender, ineffable force that elevates life into a symphony of beauty and kindness. It is the gentle art of moving through the world with an open heart, where every act of compassion—however small—echoes with divine resonance. In sowing seeds of gratitude and selfless service, we cultivate a garden of serenity and joy, wherein the light of grace illuminates our path.

10. **The Law of Sow and Reap**

Every thought, every intention, every action is a seed planted in the fertile soil of existence. This foundational law reminds us that the harvest we reap is inextricably linked to the seeds we sow. When we nurture our lives with kindness, integrity, and purpose, the universe responds in kind— blossoming into a legacy of trust, resilience, and enduring beauty.

These ten universal edicts form an intricate, interconnected framework, each one echoing the others in a celestial symphony. At their heart, the Law of Sow and Reap binds them together, a reminder that we are the architects of our destiny, crafting our lives through the choices we make and the seeds we plant.

Integrating Universal Laws into Education

If education is to be the architect of a truly awakened society, then it must evolve from a system of information delivery into a sacred space of transformation. No longer should it merely transfer knowledge from one generation to the next, but rather breathe life into timeless wisdom, embedding within each lesson the living pulse of the universe itself. To truly integrate the Universal Laws into the fabric of our collective future, education must become more than curriculum—it must become communion.

Imagine a classroom not bound by walls but expanded by intention—where the quiet rhythm of ancient truths pulses beneath the surface of every lesson, and where each subject becomes a mirror reflecting the deeper laws of life. It begins not with doctrine, but with story—narratives that awaken curiosity, spark introspection, and draw students into the wonder of their own being. Through these stories, universal principles such as balance, cause and effect, interconnectedness, and intention are not taught, but experienced. They are woven into real-world applications and everyday choices, inviting students to not only grasp their meaning, but to feel their relevance.

But the journey does not end with understanding. It must lead inward—to the realm of self-reflection. For it is in the quiet spaces, in the stillness between lessons, where true learning blooms. Here, students are guided to question: Are my actions aligned with my values? Do I live in harmony with the truth I know? These inquiries, gentle yet powerful, cultivate an inner compass—one that does not rely on external validation but on the deeper resonance of what is right, just, and whole.

From this soil of reflection rises the new seed of leadership—not the leadership of authority and control, but of vision, compassion, and moral clarity. Students no longer strive to compete or dominate, but to uplift. They become stewards of a new kind of excellence—one that serves, listens, and inspires. The emergence of such ethical leadership is not an outcome—it is a flowering, a natural result of education grounded in purpose and inner truth.

And woven through it all is the spirit of lifelong learning. Not the endless pursuit of accolades or achievements, but the quiet, enduring vow to never stop growing. In this worldview, learning is not a phase but a posture—an openness to change, a receptivity to deeper knowing, a commitment to serve. Education becomes less about climbing ladders and more about expanding horizons—an ever-evolving dance between humility and mastery.

When these universal laws are embedded into education, we are no longer merely preparing students for jobs—we are preparing them to shape the soul of society. They emerge not only as informed minds but as soul-lit beings—individuals who understand their role in the interconnected whole and who live with purpose, act with integrity, and give with joy.

In such a world, education ceases to be a means to advancement and becomes a force for awakening. It becomes the sacred breath of civilization, drawing each generation into greater harmony with itself and with all that lives. It becomes a bridge—not just between the past and the future, but between what we know and how we live.

And yet, even the most profound truths must find their voice. Wisdom, in silence, is potential. Wisdom shared, spoken, and lived—this is transformation. It is through communication, real and reverent, that these principles take root. Not just through lectures, but through conversations that touch the soul, dissolve the veil of self-importance, and invite presence.

Thus, as we step into the next chapter, we explore not only what we know, but how we share what we know. This is the essence of Real Communication—the golden thread that binds knowledge to action, that turns insight into impact, and that reminds us that truth, to be alive, must be expressed.

Chapter 16

Real Communication

In the ever-evolving tapestry of life, communication stands as the harmonic thread that binds us together, weaving meaning into our interactions and sculpting the landscapes of our relationships. Yet, in today's fragmented world, this sacred thread frays at its edges. What was once a bridge uniting minds and hearts has, in many ways, become a chasm of misunderstanding, alienation, and discord.

Once, words were vessels of wisdom, igniting revolutions, inspiring love, and healing wounds. Now, they too often wound, divide, and distort. In the digital cacophony of instant messaging, fleeting posts, and superficial exchanges, the essence of real communication is fading. But within every word, every glance, and every silence lies the potential to reconnect—to return to the art of speaking with intention, of listening with presence, and of understanding with empathy.

The Essence of Thoughtful Communication

Real communication is not merely the exchange of words, but the transmission of essence—of thought, emotion, and meaning. It is not only what is said, but how it is said, and even more deeply, the energy with which it is spoken. Within this sacred act lies a triad that governs its impact:

Words: The carriers of intention, comprising only seven percent of communication's effectiveness.

Tone: The emotional resonance, shaping thirty-eight percent of the message's influence.

Body Language: The silent symphony, conveying fifty-five percent of meaning through gestures, expressions, and posture.

Yet, in the digitized landscape where words stand alone, their burden is great. The absence of tone and gesture amplifies the need for precision, for mindfulness, and for the artistry of language to bridge the void between speaker and listener.

Imagine each word as a seed, sown in the garden of another's mind. Some words bloom into trust, connection, and understanding; others wither into discord and despair. If we are to nurture relationships and foster harmony, we must choose our words with the reverence they deserve.

The Three Categories of Language

Every word we speak—whether whispered to ourselves or shared aloud with others—falls into one of three realms:

Disempowering words are those laced with criticism, doubt, and cynicism. They erode confidence, diminish possibility, and act as silent saboteurs of growth. When directed inward, they breed insecurity and self-doubt; when projected outward, they construct barriers between people, reinforcing fear rather than fostering connection. These words often become self-fulfilling prophecies, reinforcing a limited narrative and stifling the courage needed to change.

Empowering words, by contrast, uplift, inspire, and fortify the spirit. They are the expressions of gratitude, encouragement, and vision— language that breathes life into possibilities and strengthens human bonds. Such words create the scaffolding of progress, reinforcing belief in oneself and in others, and opening new pathways for collaboration, creativity, and trust. They are the affirmations upon which transformation is built.

Polluting words are the verbal toxins of negativity, gossip, and hostility. They cloud perception, corrode meaningful dialogue, and perpetuate cycles of division. When frequently used, they contaminate the emotional atmosphere, lower vibrational frequency, and create an environment of stress and defensiveness. Over time, they drain collective energy and diminish morale, leaving communication strained and communities fractured.

To reclaim the sanctity of our interactions, we must elevate our language, shifting from disempowering and polluting words to those that enrich, enlighten, and empower. This transformation begins with self-awareness and the willingness to pause, reflect, and choose our words with care.

Self-Talk: The Foundation of Communication

The dialogue we have with ourselves is the silent architect of our external expression. Our thoughts shape our reality, defining our sense of self and our place in the world. When self-talk is negative or self-defeating, it becomes a barrier to growth and happiness.

Disempowering self-talk: "I can't do this," "I'm not good enough," or "Nothing ever works out for me" reinforces feelings of inadequacy.

Empowering self-talk: "I am capable," "I am learning and growing," or "Every challenge is an opportunity for transformation" fosters resilience and optimism.

Practicing positive self-talk is not about ignoring challenges or avoiding responsibility. To cultivate self-awareness is to refine the language of the mind. The words we whisper within become the narrative we project outward. As we elevate our internal dialogue, so too do we refine our external communication.

Empathy: The Heart of Connection

Empathy is the bridge between souls, the alchemy that transforms mere conversation into communion. Yet, in the corridors of power and the clamor of modern life, empathy is often drowned beneath the tides of ego, ambition, and societal pressures.

Research suggests that those in positions of power struggle most with empathy, their ability to attune to others dulled by dominance. But empathy is not a weakness—it is the highest form of intelligence, a force that dissolves barriers and forges unity.

To cultivate empathy, we must:

Practice Active Listening: Hear not just with the ears but with the heart. Truly listen what others are saying without planning your response.

Acknowledge Emotions: Validate the feelings of others without judgment, even if you don't fully agree with their perspective.

Release Ego: Approach conversations with humility and a genuine desire to understand.

Empathy transforms communication from a transactional exchange into a transformative experience, fostering trust, collaboration, and connection.

The Role of Tone and Body Language

While words are the vessels of meaning, tone and body language are the soul within them. A kind phrase laced with sarcasm loses its kindness, while a gentle touch or a sincere smile can communicate volumes in silence.

Tone: The emotional quality of your voice can uplift or deflate a conversation. A warm, encouraging tone invites engagement, while a harsh or dismissive tone shuts it down.

Body Language: Open gestures, eye contact, and attentive posture signal respect and interest. Conversely, crossed arms, lack of eye contact, or distracted behavior can alienate others.

Congruence: When tone and body language align with words, authenticity is established, ensuring credibility and trust.

In virtual spaces, where tone and gesture are absent, the precision of language must compensate, ensuring clarity and emotional depth in our digital interactions. Emojis, punctuation, and thoughtful phrasing can help convey emotion and intention, bridging the gap created by these platforms.

The Impact of the Arts on Communication

Art, in all its forms, is a sacred language—one that transcends grammar, dialect, and division. It speaks not only to the mind but to the soul, stirring emotions, evoking memory, and igniting a deeper connection to the shared human experience. Through the arts, we learn not just to communicate but to feel, to relate, to understand.

Music is not merely sound—it is emotion woven into vibration, the soul speaking without the need for words. Whether in the primal rhythm of drums echoing ancestral memory or the tender melody of a lullaby, music heals, inspires, and unites. Even when wordless or composed in a foreign language, it remains the purest form of communication—deeply felt, silently understood, and universally heard.

Visual art captures what language cannot contain. Paintings, sculptures, and photography serve as mirrors and windows—mirrors that reflect our innermost truths, and windows through which we glimpse the lives, cultures, and feelings of others. A single stroke of a brush can awaken empathy more powerfully than pages of prose.

Storytelling—through books, film, and theater—becomes the ancient thread that binds generations. In each story told, we step into the shoes of another, see through their eyes, and walk through their joys, sorrows, triumphs, and fears. Storytelling is not just entertainment; it is communication in its most transformative form.

Dance and movement communicate what words fail to capture. The body, when moved with intention, becomes a vessel for truth, expressing joy, grief, hope, and longing through gestures that transcend all spoken language.

And it is in the rich tapestry of these artistic expressions that the essence of real communication finds its deepest resonance.

Integrating Real Communication into Education

If knowledge is the body of education, then communication is its breath—subtle yet essential, invisible yet vital. It is through the sacred act of expression—spoken, unspoken, and deeply felt—that understanding is shared, compassion is born, and wisdom becomes a living force. To truly reimagine education, we must move beyond the sterile confines of textbooks and tests and return to the soul of learning: the ability to connect with authenticity, to listen with presence, and to speak with truth.

In the classrooms of a more awakened future, language education will not simply teach syntax or spelling—it will invite students to discover the power of words. They will explore how language can shape emotions, build or break relationships, and carry within it the seeds of healing or harm.

Moreover, communication-focused curricula can counteract the disempowering effects of rote memorization and passive learning. When students are encouraged to articulate their ideas, question assumptions, and co-create solutions, they develop not only intellectual clarity but emotional intelligence. This kind of education prepares them to navigate the complexities of a rapidly changing world with both competence and compassion.

Ultimately, thoughtful communication—rooted in empathy, enriched by the arts, and enhanced by active listening—must become a cornerstone of education reform. This requires a dual emphasis on mastering both written and verbal expression.

In the realm of writing, students should be guided to develop clarity, coherence, and creativity. Writing is not merely a method of conveying information; it is a tool for organizing thought, exploring experience, and influencing others with both reason and heart. Through essays, journaling, creative storytelling, and analytical writing, students can cultivate not only technical skill but also a lifelong love for the written word.

In spoken communication, the focus must include articulation, tone, and meaningful engagement. Speaking well empowers students to inspire trust, express ideas with confidence, and connect with diverse audiences. Public speaking exercises, debates, and performance arts such as theater allow students to present their ideas with conviction, while mindful listening practices teach them to hear deeply and respond with care.

By embracing this holistic approach—where both written and spoken communication are valued as essential life skills—we can transform not only how we teach, but how we live, lead, and relate. Through this renewed focus, we will cultivate a generation equipped not just to excel, but to elevate—dismantling the sins of education and building a world where learning uplifts, inspires, and unites us all.

A Call to Transform Communication

Real communication is more than the mere exchange of words—it is the lifeblood of human connection, the sacred pulse that fosters understanding, unity, and growth. To reclaim its essence is to restore dialogue as an art form, to wield language with wisdom, and to listen with the full presence of an open heart.

Words shape the world, carrying the power to heal or harm, to create or destroy, to unite or divide. When spoken with intention, they become bridges that span the chasms of misunderstanding. When infused with empathy, they become vessels of compassion and truth. When expressed with authenticity, they cultivate trust, collaboration, and deep human connection.

As we embark on this path, may we become artisans of conversation, sculpting every interaction with intention, grace, and sincerity. In choosing our words with reverence, in speaking with clarity and purpose, in listening with the full depth of our being, we elevate communication beyond a transactional exchange—it becomes a dance of souls, a sacred symphony of meaning and connection.

Let us speak not only to be heard but to be understood. Let us listen not only to respond but to connect. Let us foster a culture where words uplift rather than wound, where dialogue is a tool of enlightenment rather than discord, and where every conversation reflects the poetry of our highest selves.

This is where true education should lead us—toward a world where communication is not just an act but a transformative force, an intricate pathway to the heart and soul of human experience.

Chapter 17

Mastering the Written English Language in the Age of AI

The dawn of artificial intelligence and tools like ChatGPT has revolutionized the way we interact with language, offering unparalleled convenience and efficiency in written communication. These technologies can draft essays, compose emails, and even generate creative content within moments. Yet, amidst this marvel of digital ingenuity, a deeper question arises: Will humanity surrender its mastery of the written word, relinquishing the art of personal expression to the cold precision of algorithms?

In this digital era, where AI can seemingly do it all, many students may begin to neglect the importance of mastering the English language, assuming that technology will always bridge the gap. But language is more than a tool—it is the vessel of human thought, a bridge between minds and eras, a reflection of intellect, creativity, and soul. To write is to weave the unseen fabric of human consciousness into words, to shape intangible ideas into form. Without this mastery, we risk losing not only the personal satisfaction that comes from crafting one's own narrative but also the deeper connection to the ideas and emotions that make us human.

The State of Writing Skills: A Global Concern

Even before the advent of AI tools, the state of writing proficiency—particularly in the United States—revealed troubling trends. Studies have shown that a significant percentage of students, especially those in federally funded schools, struggle with basic writing skills. This is a sobering reality for a nation that prides itself on global influence and academic leadership.

If such deficiencies exist in one of the most resource-rich and technologically advanced nations, what does this imply for those with fewer educational resources, inconsistent literacy programs, and limited access to quality instruction? The challenge is even more daunting for non-English-speaking countries, where proficiency in English is often a gateway to higher education, career opportunities, and global engagement. Yet, in many of these regions, students lack the necessary infrastructure, curriculum, or support systems to master the language with confidence or clarity.

Educational disparities deepen the crisis. In underfunded schools—both in the U.S. and abroad—students are frequently taught through rote memorization rather than critical engagement. English education in developing nations is further hindered by a shortage of well-trained teachers, outdated curricula, and a rigid emphasis on mechanical correctness rather than linguistic fluidity. The erosion of grammatical precision, the shrinking of vocabulary, and the diminishing ability to craft coherent arguments are not isolated issues; they are symptoms of a deeper global malaise—the disengagement from the written word. This crisis transcends borders, threatening future generations' ability to participate in intellectual discourse, express complex ideas, and engage meaningfully in an increasingly interconnected world.

The rise of AI, while offering many benefits, threatens to exacerbate these deficiencies. In regions where educational inequalities are already stark, AI-assisted writing tools may further widen the divide between those who develop linguistic proficiency and those who become entirely dependent on automated assistance. If AI-generated content replaces active learning, non-native English speakers may never attain true fluency. This could leave them unable to engage in meaningful communication, critical thought, and creative expression, reinforcing linguistic and intellectual dependency rather than fostering independence.

The Power of Writing: More Than a Skill

Writing is far more than a mechanical process of stringing words together. It is an extension of thought, a mirror of the soul, and a record of human experience. It is the medium through which civilizations communicate across centuries, the force that preserves the wisdom of ages, and the instrument through which we define, challenge, and reshape reality. Through writing, we:

Clarify Our Thinking: Translating thoughts into words forces us to organize and refine our ideas, leading to greater mental clarity.

Preserve Knowledge: Writing serves as a record of human experience, capturing stories, insights, and discoveries for future generations.

Foster Connection: Whether through letters, essays, or stories, writing enables us to share our inner worlds and build bridges of understanding.

Empower Advocacy: A well-crafted argument has the power to inspire change, influence opinions, and mobilize communities.

Without a strong foundation in writing, individuals lose access to these transformative benefits, limiting not only their personal growth but also their ability to contribute meaningfully to society.

The Role of Education: Elevating Writing Mastery

To counteract the risks posed by over-reliance on AI and declining writing skills, schools must prioritize the teaching of English language mastery. This involves not only reinforcing foundational skills but also nurturing a love for the written word. One effective solution is the incorporation of dedicated English Language Enhancement Classes into the curriculum, integrated regularly to ensure consistent practice and meaningful engagement with language.

Components of an Effective Writing Program

1. **Vocabulary Building**:
   Students should be exposed to new words regularly, with a focus on their meanings, usage, and nuances. Interactive activities such as word games, debates, and creative challenges can make vocabulary enrichment engaging and memorable.

2. **Grammar and Syntax Mastery**:
   Clear instruction on sentence structure, punctuation, and grammatical rules is essential. Exercises should include both theoretical understanding and practical application, encouraging students to experiment with complex sentence construction.

3. **Creative Expression**:
   Writing assignments should inspire creativity, such as composing poetry, short stories, or personal essays. Journaling can serve as a tool for self-reflection, helping students connect with their emotions and thoughts.

4. **Analytical and Persuasive Writing**:
   Teach students how to construct logical arguments, analyze texts, and present their ideas persuasively. Activities like essay competitions and mock debates can sharpen critical thinking and rhetorical skills.

5. **Reading to Write**:
   Encourage extensive reading to expose students to diverse writing styles, genres, and perspectives. Discussing and analyzing literary works can inspire students to emulate effective techniques in their own writing.

The Intersection of AI and Writing

Rather than viewing AI as a threat to writing mastery, educators can position it as a complementary tool. For instance:

- **AI as a Writing Aid**: Students can use AI to enhance initial drafts or brainstorm ideas, then refine and personalize the output through their own revisions.
- **Learning Through Feedback**: AI can provide immediate feedback on grammar and syntax, helping students identify and correct errors.
- **Critical Evaluation**: Encourage students to critically analyze AI-generated content, comparing it to human-crafted writing to understand the nuances that technology cannot replicate.

However, this interplay between AI and human intelligence also reveals a deeper challenge: the growing influence of technology on creativity and individuality. The rise of digital tools opens new dimensions of interaction but also risks detaching individuals from their natural creativity and drive. Technology, when misused, can suppress curiosity and diminish the intrinsic joy of human expression.

The Lifelong Benefits of Writing Mastery

To master the art of writing is to wield one of humanity's most powerful tools—the ability to translate thought into form, emotion into expression, and vision into reality. Writing is more than a skill; it is a gateway to understanding the self, connecting with others, and shaping the world around us. For students, the mastery of written English lays the foundation for academic excellence. It refines critical thinking, sharpens analytical abilities, and empowers learners to articulate complex ideas with clarity, structure, and nuance. Whether composing a persuasive essay, crafting a research paper, or engaging in reflective journaling, writing becomes the vessel through which the mind is both disciplined and liberated.

Beyond the classroom, writing is an indispensable key to professional success. In an era where clear, impactful communication is the currency of leadership, innovation, and influence, those who can express themselves effectively stand out. From proposals and reports to emails and speeches, the ability to write with intention and eloquence opens doors, builds trust, and inspires action.

In the digital landscape that now defines our age, the written word has become our primary mode of interaction. In a world of emails, social media posts, blogs, and digital forums, writing shapes how we are seen, heard, and understood. It is through the written word that reputations are built, movements are sparked, and ideas travel across continents in the blink of an eye. Writing well in this sphere ensures not only personal credibility but also the power to influence thought, challenge injustice, and inspire change.

Yet perhaps most profoundly, writing mastery enables us to engage with the world as conscious, compassionate global citizens. It allows us to voice our truth, share our stories, and contribute to the ongoing dialogue of humanity. Through writing, we preserve memory, imagine futures, and advocate for those whose voices are often unheard. We become participants in shaping not only our own destinies but also the collective journey of society.

To write is to leave a mark—not just on paper, but on hearts, minds, and the unfolding narrative of our shared human experience. It is a sacred act of presence, a declaration of thought, and a bridge between solitude and solidarity. The pen may seem simple, but in the hands of one who has mastered its power, it becomes a beacon that lights the way for generations to come.

The Role of Real Intelligence (RI) and ONENESS in Writing Mastery

The intersection of Artificial Intelligence (AI) and writing mastery presents not just a technical challenge but a philosophical one. As machines become more sophisticated in generating text, the question arises: What separates human intelligence from artificial intelligence? The answer lies in Real Intelligence (RI)—the innate, intuitive, and deeply connected intelligence that defines human consciousness. Unlike AI, which processes information without experience or emotion, RI is fueled by creativity, intuition, and the ability to weave meaning from existence itself.

At the heart of RI is Oneness, the unifying force behind all thought, creation, and understanding. This divine essence reflects the interconnected nature of human consciousness, transcending mechanical processing to infuse writing with depth, soul, and authenticity. It is the difference between a machine-generated essay that follows patterns and a human-crafted narrative that evokes emotion, provokes thought, and fosters connection.

When students cultivate Real Intelligence (RI), they are not merely learning to write—they are learning to think, feel, and express in a way that resonates with the deeper truths of human experience. They become architects of language, shaping words not as mere tools but as vessels of meaning that bridge minds and hearts. This is where AI, if guided properly, can complement rather than replace human creativity. By leveraging AI as a tool while nurturing RI, students can transcend formulaic responses and produce work that embodies originality, vision, and profound insight.

A Call to Action: Reclaiming the Art of Writing

Technology holds the potential to elevate humanity, but without a unifying principle, it can just as easily lead us astray. The rise of AI and digital tools presents both challenges and opportunities. To navigate this landscape, students must not abandon the foundational skill of writing but rather embrace it as a source of empowerment.

By incorporating robust English language enhancement programs into education, we can ensure that the next generation possesses the tools to think critically, communicate effectively, and contribute creatively. Mastery of the written word is not merely an academic requirement; it is a lifelong asset.

In a world increasingly mediated by technology, it is the human touch—the ability to infuse words with thought, emotion, and purpose—that will set individuals apart. Through deliberate practice, thoughtful instruction, and a commitment to continuous learning, we can preserve the art of writing and inspire students to wield it as a force for connection, understanding, and transformation.

Chapter 18

The Re-Alignment of Our Core Character

Earlier in this book, I described how our core character is formed at a very early stage of our life, often by the age of seven. Now the obvious question is: Are we bound by this early conditioning, forever tethered to a self we had little role in shaping, or do we possess the power to transform, to evolve beyond the subconscious scripts imprinted upon us?

It is often believed that reading a soul-searching book, attending a transformative workshop, or experiencing a life-altering incident can lead us to rethink our core beliefs, fundamental values, and deeply embedded habits. Such moments can awaken within us a new understanding, revealing the timeless universal truths that have always surrounded us yet remained unseen. One of the most profound realizations in this journey is that of Oneness—the truth that we are not separate, isolated beings but integral threads woven into the vast, boundless tapestry of existence. It is through this recognition that we can realign our core character and transform our lives in unimaginable ways. To illustrate this point, let me share a real-life story.

A Transformative Encounter: The Power of Realignment

Years ago, I was approached by members of my Sikh community to sponsor a radio program broadcasting Sabad-kirtan (spiritual songs and prayers) every Saturday morning. I agreed and was introduced to Ray Somich, the owner of a radio station in Ohio, to discuss the program details. What began as a brief logistical meeting unfolded into a dialogue that would change my path forever.

Ray, intrigued by my perspectives, suggested that we collaborate on a talk show. Though hesitant at first, I agreed, and in 1995, we launched a weekly show called Stress-Free Living. Our conversations were unscripted, spontaneous explorations of universal wisdom, flowing naturally as though guided by a force beyond ourselves.

Four months into the show, doubt crept in. Who was I to speak on such profound topics? Was I truly qualified? My inner voice whispered uncertainty, urging me to step away before my inadequacies were exposed. Just as I was about to surrender to these doubts, a phone call changed everything.

A woman's voice, tinged with urgency, reached me: "I am dying. Will you fulfill a wish for this dying lady?" Shocked, I listened as she recounted her story. Diagnosed with advanced breast cancer, she had become bitter, angry, and disillusioned. Then, one day, her son played a recording of our show for her. "It changed everything," she said. "Your words brought me peace, gratitude, and a renewed sense of life. I live fully now, despite my limited time." Her plea was simple yet powerful—continue the show.

In that moment, I understood something profound: we are but vessels for a higher wisdom, conduits for the universal truth of Oneness. The radio show was not about me; it was about the messages flowing through me, messages meant to uplift and transform others. With renewed clarity, I continued, and as of July 2024, Stress-Free Living has completed thirty years of production, touching countless lives.

The Science of Transformation: Lessons from Epigenetics and Nature

Our core character, once thought to be a fixed construct, is in fact a dynamic, evolving force shaped by the interplay of genetics and experience. The emerging field of epigenetics reveals that our environment, choices, and even thoughts influence the very expression of our genes.

This dismantles the outdated notion of an unchangeable identity, reinforcing the idea that who we become is not solely dictated by our past but by our willingness to realign and evolve.

For centuries, scientists believed our genetic blueprint was set at birth, dictating behaviors, strengths, and limitations. However, modern research tells a different story—one where our life experiences imprint chemical markers on our DNA, activating or silencing genes in response to love, stress, trauma, education, and social interactions. The early years of life are particularly influential in this process, as the neural pathways that shape cognition, emotional intelligence, and resilience are formed during this critical period.

If genes are the notes on a musical score, then epigenetics is the conductor determining how life's melody is played. This means that while our childhood environment shapes us profoundly, we are never truly bound by it. Like glass reshaped in a furnace or iron forged in fire, we, too, can be remolded through conscious effort, self-awareness, and deliberate action.

Embracing Challenges as Gifts

Adversity is the furnace in which transformation is kindled. Yet, too often, we view challenges as burdens rather than catalysts for growth. To realign our core character, we must shift our perspective:

1. **Accept Challenges with Gratitude**: Recognize that every difficulty carries within it a lesson meant to elevate us. Instead of asking, "Why me?" ask, "What is this teaching me?"
2. **Cultivate Perseverance and Patience**: Growth is not instantaneous. Just as a tree takes years to bear fruit, deep transformation requires time and conscious effort.
3. **Align with Universal Wisdom**: Every challenge is part of a greater design, a force leading us closer to the realization of our true identity.

Daily Practices for Realignment

The realignment of our core character does not happen in a single moment of epiphany; it is cultivated through consistent, intentional practice. Here is a simple yet transformative exercise:

The Morning Reflection Exercise

1. **Create a Quiet Space**: Find a peaceful place where you can sit or stand comfortably, undisturbed.
2. **Begin with Deep Breathing**: Inhale deeply for four counts, hold for two counts, and exhale slowly for eight counts. Repeat for five minutes, allowing your mind to center.
3. **Reflect on Your Body's Miracles**: With your eyes closed or gazing softly at a natural object, silently acknowledge the intricate perfection of your being—from your beating heart to your perceptive senses. Recognize your body not merely as flesh and bone, but as a sacred vessel—a gift that carries something far greater than the physical form.
4. **Internalize Gratitude**: Close your eyes and immerse yourself in the feeling of gratitude—not just for your own life, but for the interconnected existence of all beings. Let this gratitude permeate every cell of your being.
5. **Embrace Oneness**: Visualize the universal force that animates you, recognizing it as the same energy that flows through all living things. Let this awareness dissolve the illusion of separation.

The Role of Educators and Parents in Realignment

True transformation does not occur in isolation; it is deeply influenced by the environments that shape us. Educators and parents are the architects of this transformation, serving as the guiding forces that instill the foundation upon which children build their understanding of self and the world. If they are to nurture adaptability, resilience, and growth in the next generation, they must first embrace these principles themselves.

A teacher who perceives learning as an ever-evolving journey rather than a static destination, and a parent who understands that character is not rigid but responsive to growth—these individuals set the stage for lifelong transformation. When they embody resilience, open-mindedness, and emotional intelligence, children absorb these qualities not as distant ideals but as natural ways of being.

The role of educators extends beyond imparting knowledge—it is about fostering independent thought, critical inquiry, and emotional intelligence. In an education system that often prioritizes memorization over meaningful exploration, teachers who inspire curiosity, facilitate open-ended discussions, and encourage self-reflection create fertile ground for students to develop into adaptable, self-aware individuals.

Similarly, parents who lead with authenticity, engage in meaningful dialogue, and practice emotional resilience model the transformative power of self-awareness. A home must be more than a place of instruction; it must be an incubator of evolving consciousness, where children witness realignment as an ongoing process rather than a singular event.

When educators and parents embrace transformation as a lifelong journey, they create an ecosystem where children see growth as an intrinsic part of life. The most profound lessons are not those dictated through authority, but those demonstrated through lived experience. By embracing personal evolution, they empower a new generation not just to accept change, but to actively seek it as a means of self-discovery and fulfillment.

True transformation begins not just with individuals but within the environments that nurture them. Educators and parents must first embrace realignment within themselves before they can effectively guide children toward the same realization. A teacher who understands the fluidity of personal growth, a parent who recognizes the malleability of character—these figures become beacons of possibility, illuminating the path for the next generation.

When adults model adaptability, resilience, and an openness to change, children absorb these qualities not as abstract ideals but as lived truths. If teachers approach education with a mindset of growth rather than rigid instruction, and if parents foster environments where questioning, exploration, and transformation are encouraged, then the potential for realignment expands beyond the individual— it becomes a shared journey of enlightenment.

The Infinite Potential of Realignment

We are not bound by the shadows of our past. In aligning with universal wisdom, we unlock the ability to live authentically, serve selflessly, and inspire transformation in others. When we embrace the path of continuous realignment, we step into the infinite potential of who we are meant to be—individuals who live with clarity, act with compassion, and embody the timeless truth whispered by the forgotten language of the soul—the language that remembers we are one.

Thus, transformation is not a distant dream; it is a daily practice. The power to reshape our character, to redefine our story, and to illuminate the lives of others lies within us. All that is required is the willingness to step into the fire of change, trusting that in its heat, we will emerge stronger, purer, and more aligned with the essence of who we truly are.

Chapter 19

The State of Modern Worldly Education

Modern education is often heralded as the great equalizer, the foundation upon which individuals build their understanding of the world. It arms students with knowledge, analytical tools, and specialized skills, preparing them to navigate the complexities of an ever-changing society. It equips us to question, to create, to innovate—to construct bridges, cure diseases, design technology, and contribute to economic progress. And yet, despite its undeniable value, modern education remains deeply flawed, for it sharpens the intellect while often neglecting the soul. It arms the mind but leaves the heart untended. It teaches us how to succeed, yet rarely asks us what success truly means.

This incompleteness arises from an inherent limitation: modern education is largely transactional rather than transformational. It is structured to provide information, but not wisdom; it fosters ambition, but not self-awareness; it prepares students for a career, but not necessarily for a life of meaning. The system is designed to fill minds with facts, formulas, and theories, yet it rarely nurtures the deeper inquiries that shape a fulfilling existence: Who am I? How am I designed? What is my purpose? What am I here to give?

The Challenges of Modern World: The Sins of Education

The sins of our current education system are not abstract concerns; they are deeply embedded realities that shape the trajectory of our society. Instead of awakening curiosity and unlocking human potential, our institutions often suppress them. Instead of fostering wisdom, they emphasize mere knowledge. Instead of nurturing critical thinking, they reward compliance. The result is a system that repeatedly fails to:

- Inspire lifelong curiosity and intellectual engagement.
- Cultivate genuine critical thinking and independent reasoning.
- Recognize and nurture individual talents and passions.
- Unleash the boundless creative and spiritual potential within each student.
- Foster integrity, ethical discernment, and moral responsibility.
- Instill habits essential for true success and holistic well-being.
- Equip individuals with lifelong skills to lead with compassion, confidence, and clarity of purpose.

Instead of empowering students to explore their uniqueness, education forces them into rigid molds, prioritizing conformity over originality, competition over collaboration, and superficial achievement over profound understanding. It upholds a distorted vision of success—one measured by grades, degrees, and accolades rather than depth of insight and contribution to the greater good. It reinforces a self-serving question—"What's in it for me?"—while neglecting the deeper question: "What am I here to give?"

Even the most prestigious institutions, with their abundant resources and distinguished faculty, cannot remedy this flaw as long as education remains disconnected from the fundamental truth of human existence—the realization that we are more than our intellect, our nationality, our credentials, or our status. Without an inner compass, education becomes a tool wielded by fear, greed, and the myth of individual supremacy. A system that should uplift humanity instead becomes the very force that divides and exploits it.

The ultimate sin of this flawed education system is that it conditions individuals to adopt a false identity—one that defines worth by external validation rather than intrinsic value. Consequently, we develop erroneous perceptions, make misguided conclusions, and set forth on paths that lead to individual and societal disillusionment. Left unchallenged, this trajectory will continue toward an inevitable crisis of purpose, meaning, and self-destruction.

The Crisis of Superficial Knowledge

At its core, modern education is driven by external benchmarks—grades, degrees, certifications, and standardized tests. Students are conditioned to memorize and regurgitate information without fully comprehending its deeper implications. They are rewarded for their ability to conform to established norms, to excel in predetermined curricula, and to compete in a system that measures intelligence through a narrow, often outdated, framework. But does this approach foster genuine understanding? Or does it merely create individuals who are highly skilled at following instructions yet lack the ability to think independently, to reflect deeply, or to cultivate inner wisdom?

The modern academic system prioritizes what to think over how to think. It celebrates those who can recall information, yet does little to encourage introspection or original thought. Knowledge, when disconnected from wisdom, becomes fragmented—disjointed pieces of information that serve practical purposes but fail to provide a holistic understanding of life's greater purpose. A student may master physics, economics, or medicine, but without a foundational understanding of their own consciousness and the interconnectedness of all life, their education remains incomplete.

A System Focused on Competition, Not Contribution

Education today is structured around competition. Students are taught to view life as a race—one in which success is defined by outperforming others, securing higher grades, obtaining prestigious degrees, and entering elite institutions. This relentless emphasis on comparison fosters insecurity, anxiety, and a scarcity mindset.

It conditions individuals to seek validation externally rather than cultivating a deep, intrinsic sense of purpose.

Instead of asking, "How can I contribute?" students are conditioned to ask, "How can I get ahead?" Instead of being encouraged to discover their unique strengths and passions, they are pressured to conform to societal expectations—often choosing careers based on market demand rather than personal alignment. The result? A generation of individuals who may achieve material success yet feel an inexplicable emptiness, a lingering question that remains unanswered: Is this all there is?

Reinventing the Classroom

Imagine a classroom where education is not confined within the rigid structures of standardized tests and rote memorization, but instead flourishes as a dynamic symphony of intellect, creativity, and soulful inquiry. A classroom where students are not mere vessels to be filled with information, but luminous minds sculpted through the harmonization of knowledge, purpose, and inner wisdom. Imagine a world where the walls of learning spaces breathe with inspiration, where curiosity is the guiding force, and where education is no longer a system to endure but an odyssey of transformation.

To reinvent the classroom is to redefine the very essence of what it means to be a student—a seeker of truth, a cultivator of wisdom, a beacon of service. It is to dissolve the archaic barriers between subjects and illuminate the profound interconnectedness of all fields of thought. It is to embrace not only the quantifiable intelligence of the mind but the immeasurable depth of the heart and spirit. Such an evolution of learning would be rooted in principles that foster the highest expression of human potential:

Mindfulness as the Foundation: Each day begins with mindfulness—an intentional moment of presence, stillness, and reflection. Students learn to navigate the storm of modern life with the compass of inner tranquility, developing clarity, resilience, and a deeper connection to their authentic selves. With this foundation, learning ceases to be a frantic pursuit of achievement and instead becomes an act of devotion to self-mastery.

Service as the Purpose: Education, at its core, must transcend the individual and ripple outward into the fabric of society. Imagine a learning environment where students engage in service-based projects, translating theoretical knowledge into tangible impact. Whether through environmental restoration, social advocacy, or mentorship programs, students find meaning not in grades, but in the lives they touch and uplift. In doing so, they come to understand that true success is measured not by accumulation, but by contribution.

Interdisciplinary Integration: No longer shall subjects be treated as isolated silos of information. Instead, let us weave a curriculum that mirrors the rich, interwoven tapestry of reality. Science and philosophy converge to explore the mysteries of existence. Mathematics and music resonate together in the language of patterns. Literature and history intertwine to unveil the stories of humanity's collective journey. In such an approach, knowledge becomes alive, pulsating with meaning and infinite possibilities.

Wisdom Over Mere Knowledge: An education system that prioritizes wisdom over mere intellectual accumulation fosters a new breed of lifelong learners—individuals who not only seek truth but discern its application for the greater good. Wisdom is the alchemy of knowledge and virtue, and without it, even the most advanced intellect remains blind. It is through this elevation of learning that we transform students into visionaries, not just professionals; into creators, not just consumers; into leaders who carry the torch of enlightenment for future generations.

A Call to Transcend

The hour is ripe for transformation. The traditional model of education is crumbling under the weight of its own obsolescence, and in its place, we must build a sanctuary of learning that nurtures the whole human being—mind, heart, and spirit. It is time for educators to become guides of enlightenment, for students to embrace learning as a sacred responsibility, and for parents and policymakers to reimagine education as an ecosystem of human flourishing.

To continue along the path of fragmented, soulless learning is to perpetuate a cycle of division, competition, and hollow success. But to embark on this higher path—to center education around the principle of adding the highest value in every endeavor—is to awaken the dormant brilliance within each student. It is to forge a future where knowledge serves wisdom, where achievement serves humanity, and where learning is a lifelong devotion to the betterment of all.

Chapter 20

What Makes a Lifelong, Highest-Value-Adding Student?

We often hear that money drives the world, as many place their bets on love, power, commerce, or the magnetic pull of ambition. But beneath these visible forces lies a quieter, more insidious current: insecurity. This invisible thread weaves itself into the fabric of human life—shaping decisions, coloring relationships, and quietly defining the very structure of society. It is the silent architect of our fears, the unseen hand that molds our ambitions, the shadowed voice whispering that we are never quite enough. It compels us to seek validation, to measure worth against fleeting standards, and to prioritize external achievement over inner fulfillment.

Insecurity: The Unseen Force Shaping Society and Education

Insecurity has seeped into every facet of our world—from politics to education, from the boardroom to the classroom. It fuels behaviors that prioritize control over courage, dominance over dialogue, superficial success over genuine fulfillment. And nowhere is this more evident than in our education system, which, instead of fostering boundless curiosity, often mirrors the anxieties of the society it serves.

Education, meant to be the liberator of the human mind, instead becomes a factory of conformity, where:

Books are banned and censored to protect fragile illusions rather than challenge minds.

Curricula are stripped of diverse perspectives to maintain a "safe" and palatable narrative.

Critical thinking is diminished, replaced by a system that rewards mere memorization and passive compliance. Standardized tests are placed on pedestals, while personal growth, character, and wisdom are relegated to afterthoughts.

Rather than cultivating individuals who are fearless in their pursuit of truth, education often breeds hesitation, conditioning students to fear failure, doubt the unfamiliar and resist what is unique, and seek validation through achievement rather than understanding. The pursuit of knowledge is reduced to a mere checklist, robbing students of the joy of intellectual discovery.

But what is the antidote to this insecurity? It is the cultivation of a lifelong, highest-value-adding student—one who is not shaped by fear, but by purpose; not driven by validation, but by contribution. Such a student is not merely an academic achiever, but a conscious creator, a lighthouse in a storm of mediocrity. They are not reactive to the world's demands, but generative in their service to it.

The Cost of Insecurity: A Mediocre Society

When insecurity dictates the trajectory of a civilization, mediocrity becomes not just an outcome but a silent creed—a settling for less, not out of contentment, but out of fear. Mediocrity is not mere ordinariness; it is the slow decay of aspiration, the stagnation of the human spirit caused by an unwillingness to step beyond the familiar, to confront the unknown, to dare toward greatness.

It manifests in superficial accomplishments masquerading as genuine progress, where appearances are applauded while true innovation remains suppressed. A society begins to confuse accolades with excellence, satisfied with ornamentation over transformation, mistaking recognition for real impact. Leadership, once envisioned as a beacon to uplift and unify, turns inward—serving its own image rather than the collective good—trading vision for vanity, and compromising integrity for influence.

Our schools bear the deepest scars of this decline. Institutions once entrusted with nurturing boundless potential have become factories of uniformity. The sacred act of learning has been reduced to a transactional routine—an exercise in memorization, obedience, and external validation, rather than the awakening of insight and wisdom.

Teachers, burdened by bureaucracy, find their flame for illumination dimmed by a system that values efficiency over enlightenment. Students, shackled by rigid expectations, are trained to comply, to color inside the lines of convention rather than to paint boldly with the hues of imagination. Creativity is not nurtured; it is stifled. Individuality is not celebrated; it is subdued. Curiosity is not encouraged; it is controlled.

And yet, the true tragedy is this: we do not even mourn the loss. The erosion of human potential does not announce itself with calamity. It is a quiet suffocation—a gradual, imperceptible dimming of the inner flame. It does not destroy in a moment; it withers over time, until all that remains is a world of silenced dreams, dulled spirits, and a humanity that has forgotten the brilliance it was born to embody.

Uniqueness: The Missed Miracle

Nature is a constant celebration of uniqueness. No two leaves are identical, no two snowflakes mirror each other, and no two human beings share the same fingerprints. Yet our education system, blind to this wonder, insists on treating students as interchangeable units, measuring them against uniform standards rather than nurturing their individuality. This rigid model does not merely diminish the individual—it impoverishes society by depriving it of the diversity of thought and perspective necessary for innovation, growth, and wisdom.

Ironically, while each of us is unique, we are also bound by a shared essence—the universal energy that animates all life. To recognize this is to step beyond the self-serving question of personal gain to the higher inquiry, "What am I here to give?" The student who embraces this question embarks on a journey not just of learning, but of transformation.

A Blueprint for Transformation

If we are to break free from the cycle of insecurity and mediocrity, education must be reimagined as more than a mere system of instruction—it must become a catalyst for empowerment. It must transcend its role as a mechanism of conformity and evolve into a force of liberation, where students are not confined to predefined molds but awakened to the boundless potential within them. No longer just a pathway to careers, education must be a gateway to self-discovery, service, and mastery—an odyssey where students do not merely accumulate knowledge but uncover purpose, forging lives of meaning, contribution, and excellence.

Cultivating Inner Confidence: Before students can excel outwardly, they must first believe in their intrinsic worth. When self-worth is tethered to external validation—grades, approval, accolades—students become prisoners of expectation rather than pioneers of their own destiny. To transform this, education must shift from a system of judgment to a sanctuary of self-exploration. It must integrate practices that nurture resilience, gratitude, and self-awareness, allowing students to view failure not as a verdict, but as a vital stepping stone on the path to mastery. In this atmosphere, confidence is not fabricated—it is unearthed.

Nurturing Unique Talents: Education should not aim to mold students into a single, standardized ideal but to honor their inherent design. Every mind is a singular universe, every soul carrying a distinct purpose—so why do we teach them as if they are the same? The shift must be from one-size-fits-all education to personalized learning journeys that celebrate curiosity, passion, and originality.

Genius must no longer be measured solely by tests but by the courage to think differently, to express creatively, and to explore innovatively. In honoring uniqueness, we unleash brilliance.

Building Emotional Intelligence: For far too long, education has exalted intellect and sidelined emotion. Yet knowledge devoid of empathy is inert, and intelligence without compassion can be perilous. We must elevate emotional intelligence to the same pedestal as academic acumen. Let us foster school cultures where kindness, empathy, and ethical decision-making are considered strengths, not side notes. Let us teach students not merely how to argue their positions, but how to understand another's pain. For wisdom is not the ability to win debates—it is the power to build bridges.

Encouraging Lifelong Curiosity: Today's education often turns learning into performance—a chase for credentials, a sprint toward economic survival. But true education must be less about outcomes and more about awe. We must inspire students to ask the timeless questions of existence, to dive into inquiry not for grades but for meaning. Shift the focus from performance-based learning to curiosity-driven exploration. Let education be seen not as a task that ends with graduation but as a lifelong pilgrimage of discovery. For when learning is driven by the joy of wonder, students don't just succeed—they flourish.

Embedding Purpose and Service: Imagine if the central question in education was not, "What can you achieve?" but "What can you give?" Success must be redefined—not as the amassing of accolades, but as the depth of one's contribution to the greater good. Let curricula include service-learning that connects knowledge to real-world impact. Let fulfillment be rooted not in self-interest, but in selfless giving. In the end, the truest measure of education is not how much knowledge was acquired, but how much wisdom was applied; not how many achievements were obtained, but how many lives were touched; not how high one climbed, but how deeply one understood.

And what happens when students are never asked these deeper questions? When education becomes a checklist instead of a calling? We witness the quiet epidemic of disengagement—detachment, apathy, and resignation. Purpose becomes peripheral, and potential lies dormant. But when students are not merely taught but awakened—when their inner spark is seen, nurtured, and called forth—everything changes.

Such a transformation is not theoretical; it has been lived. One powerful example unfolded at Collinwood High School in Cleveland, where for far too long, students had been seen as statistics in a struggling system rather than as souls with untapped potential.

This transformation was catalyzed by Project Love, a non-profit organization founded by Stuart Muszynski as part of the Values-in-Action Foundation. At the time, I served as Chairman of the Board, deeply involved in its initiatives to awaken students to their true essence and redefine the very purpose of education.

Case Study: Collinwood High School and Project Love

The Turnaround of a Failing School

In the heart of Cleveland, where the walls of Collinwood High School bore the weight of forgotten dreams and the air was thick with resignation, a silent crisis unfolded. The corridors, once meant to echo with youthful ambition, had become passageways of disillusionment. The numbers painted a grim reality—less than 45 percent of the girls graduated, their aspirations crumbling beneath the weight of generational hardship. Teenage pregnancy loomed at a staggering 30 percent, an unspoken sentence that redirected futures before they had the chance to begin. Drugs were not merely an escape; they were an accepted companion, claiming nearly 70 percent of the students in their grip. And beyond these walls? A future of uncertainty—only 2 percent of students ever reached the threshold of a college education.

The system had failed them. But what if the failure was not in resources, not in facilities, not in textbooks or teaching methods? What if the greatest missing piece was something more fundamental—something unseen, yet more powerful than anything that could be measured by standardized tests?

This question ignited a bold experiment that sought not to reform education with bureaucracy, but to transform lives through a simple, radical truth: the awakening of the self. It was a journey, not of curriculum adjustments, but of consciousness expansion—an endeavor to remind students that they were not defined by their circumstances, but by the limitless potential within them.

Project Love introduced a program called "Believe to Achieve." At its core was not new infrastructure, not financial handouts, not academic overhauls—but something far more profound: a reclamation of identity.

For four years, a Project Love counselor walked alongside these students, not as an authority figure, but as a guardian of their potential. They met weekly, and for those in crisis, the counselor was available 24/7—a steady presence in lives too often marked by inconsistency and neglect. Trust was not demanded; it was earned. And once it was won, the transformation began.

The process started with questions—questions designed not to impose knowledge, but to unravel the unseen chains that had bound them for so long:

- Does your color or gender define you?
- Does your past define you?
- How do you define your real core strengths?
- What is really holding you back from achieving success?
- How do you define true success?
- Do you live your knowledge or your habits?
- Who controls your happiness?

Each question was a doorway, leading them deeper into the forgotten chambers of their own being. And once the questions had unsettled their assumptions, the deeper truths were revealed:

- Who are you?
- How are you designed?
- What is your true purpose in life?

Something within them stirred. For perhaps the first time, they saw themselves not through the lens of limitations, but through the limitless nature of their own existence. Life was no longer a series of conditions to endure, but a gift to be embraced. They were not just bodies navigating a broken system, but luminous beings capable of forging their own paths. They were not statistics; they were forces of change. And as this realization took root, the transformation became visible—not just in their words, but in their actions.

- Discipline replaced disorder.
- Respect became second nature—not just for authority, but for themselves.
- Their eyes, once dulled by despair, now gleamed with the quiet fire of purpose.

It was not magic. It was not luck. It was the undeniable truth that once a person awakens to their intrinsic worth, they rise—not because they are told to, but because they finally see that they were never meant to remain bound. The results spoke for themselves, etched in numbers that told the story of souls reclaimed:

	Before	After
Graduation rate	45%	85%
Pregnancy rate	30%	0%
Illicit drug use	70%	10%
College enrollment	2%	60%

No new buildings were erected. No teachers were replaced. No vast sums of money were poured into infrastructure. The world loves to believe that change requires grand investment, complex strategy, and institutional reform. But this revolution came at almost no cost. It required only one thing: the recognition of true identity. And yet, while Collinwood's story is nothing short of extraordinary, it also stands as an indictment—a damning reflection of the larger failure of modern education.

Consider this: America—the most influential nation on the globe—invests over a trillion dollars annually in education, a sum unparalleled in history. And yet, despite this staggering expenditure, over 1.2 million students drop out of high school every year, slipping through the cracks of a system designed to educate but failing to empower.

And what of those who do graduate? Those who navigate the system, earn degrees, and enter the professional world? They often find themselves burdened with crushing student debt, entangled in a corporate culture that prioritizes profit over ethics, ambition over integrity, and competition over contribution. Many become the architects of white-collar crime, economic disparity, and systemic corruption, fueling a society where greed masquerades as success and self-interest infiltrates every institution—from finance to politics, from healthcare to law.

We pour billions into the external mechanisms of education—state-of-the-art buildings, standardized testing, digital tools—yet neglect the one thing that truly matters: the internal awakening that fosters true leaders, true visionaries, and true contributors. But here—at Collinwood—without money, without academic reform, without structural change, something miraculous happened: The students became better students—not because they were forced to, but because they had found their own reason to rise.

And so, the question remains: Are we willing to reimagine education—not as an institution of facts, but as a cathedral of self-realization? Are we bold enough to shift the paradigm—not by pouring more money into the system, but by awakening the spirit within each student? For in the end, the world does not need more graduates chasing success. It needs more awakened minds shaping a better future.

A Call to Redefine Education: Awakening Minds, Igniting Souls

Education, as it stands, is a pale shadow of what it was always meant to be. It has become a machine, producing minds that excel in logic but falter in wisdom, that accumulate knowledge but remain empty of purpose. It has become a path that guides students toward careers but not toward meaning, that teaches them how to make a living but not how to truly live. The time has come to redefine education—not as an institution, but as a living force, a sacred journey of awakening, refinement, and service.

For true education is not the filling of a vessel but the kindling of a fire—a fire that burns with the desire to know oneself, to understand one's place in the grand symphony of existence, to uplift and illuminate. It must go beyond the memorization of facts and formulas, beyond the pursuit of grades and degrees, and instead become a quest for higher truth. It must instill not just intelligence, but wisdom; not just ambition, but reverence; not just success, but significance.

We must break the chains that bind learning to mere memorization and shallow achievement, and instead set it free—to inspire, to elevate, to liberate. Education must no longer be confined to classrooms, textbooks, and examination halls, but must stretch beyond these walls to embrace the full spectrum of human potential. It must be a revelation, not merely an instruction; a transformation, not merely a preparation.

And at the heart of this evolution lies the most sacred inquiry of all:
Who am I?
How am I designed?
What is my purpose?
What am I here to give?

For an education that fails to ask these questions is an education that fails to awaken the soul.

The Educator as a Catalyst for Transformation

To truly transform education, we must first redefine the role of the educator. Yet, this role is not confined to the walls of a classroom. It extends far beyond teachers—it begins in the home, with the first and most enduring educators: parents. For long before a child sets foot in a school, they are absorbing the lessons of life from their caregivers— through words spoken, through actions observed, through unspoken values passed down from generation to generation. Education is not solely an institutional responsibility; it is a collective calling.

A teacher must no longer be a mere dispenser of information but a guardian of potential, a guide to the uncharted territories of the mind and spirit. Likewise, a parent must no longer see their role as one of control and instruction, but of nurturing and illumination. Both must recognize that their task is not simply to prepare a child to survive in the world, but to awaken within them the capacity to shape it.

Yet, to achieve this transformation, we must first confront an uncomfortable truth: We, as educators, as parents, as mentors, have inherited a flawed system of thinking. Having gone through the same standardized education ourselves, we unknowingly absorbed its most insidious flaw—the mindset of "What's in it for me?" rather than "What am I here to give?" This self-centered approach to success has seeped into every aspect of our lives, even into our most intimate relationships—marriage, family, and friendships. It has shaped the way we teach, the way we lead, and the way we raise our children.

Thus, the transformation of education must begin with us. If teachers and parents remain trapped in the same transactional mindset they unknowingly inherited, they will unconsciously pass it down to the next generation. But if they evolve, if they awaken to their own higher purpose, they will become true catalysts of transformation. They will break the cycle. They will lead not by authority, but by example.

A true educator—whether in the classroom or at home—sees beyond grades, beyond achievements, beyond societal expectations. They recognize that within each child burns an indestructible light, a singular genius waiting to be discovered. Their role is not to force conformity but to guide each soul toward the fearless pursuit of its highest calling.

Imagine a world where students are not conditioned to compete but to collaborate. Where learning is not driven by fear of failure but by the joy of discovery. Where imagination is not stifled but celebrated; where failures are not a source of shame but a testament to growth.

Such an education does not merely prepare students for the world as it is—it prepares them to create the world as it ought to be.

Imagining a World of ONENESS

A world that fully embraces the paradigm of Oneness is a world that has transcended the illusion of separateness—a world where education is no longer a race for individual achievement, but a collective awakening. It is a world where knowledge is not hoarded but shared; where wisdom is not commodified but lived; where learning is not confined to institutions but interwoven into the very fabric of existence.

But the reality of Oneness is not an abstract ideal; it is woven into the very origins of humanity. The story of Adam and Eve is not merely a tale of creation but a profound revelation of the inseparable nature of man and woman. Eve was not created as a separate being, but from a part of Adam himself—from his rib, from within his own body. She was not formed from the dust as he was, but drawn from him, symbolizing an eternal unity that predates all divisions. They were two, yet they were always one.

This truth was meant to illuminate the foundation of human relationships. It was not just a story of the first man and woman—it was a blueprint for all relationships that followed. The unity of Adam and Eve was meant to be the first reflection of divine Oneness in the world. A love so complete that it did not seek to possess or dominate but to honor and uplift. A recognition that to cherish the other is to cherish the self, to harm the other is to harm the self.

But over time, humanity forgot this fundamental truth. Instead of embracing their shared essence, men and women became adversaries, competitors, striving for dominance rather than unity. The original harmony that was meant to shape families and mold future generations was lost to discord, and from that loss, a fragmented world was born—one that bred division, conflict, and self-interest.

If we are to restore Oneness, it must begin where it was first broken—in the home, in the sacred union between man and woman. For parents are the first educators, and their love, or lack thereof, shapes the consciousness of their children long before any school does. Children learn not through words alone, but through the energy of the home, through the unspoken language of how their parents love, honor, and acknowledge each other.

Imagine a world where parents embody Oneness—where a child does not grow up witnessing competition between mother and father, but harmony; not power struggles, but mutual respect; not conditions, but unconditional love. When a father cherishes the mother, he teaches his sons how to honor women and his daughters how to receive love with dignity. When a mother respects the father, she teaches her daughters strength through grace and her sons how to become men who uplift rather than suppress.

In such a home, education begins not with words, but with being. Children absorb their first lessons not from textbooks, but from the way love is exchanged between their parents. They do not need to be told what Oneness means; they see it in the way their parents serve one another selflessly, forgive without resentment, uplift without expectation. They learn that to love is not to seek one's own gain, but to give freely, knowing that in giving, one receives.

From such a foundation, the illusion of separateness dissolves—race, class, nationality—outdated divisions fade before the realization that we are all bound by the same breath, the same energy, the same eternal source of life.

In such a world, learning becomes a shared journey—where students, teachers, and parents evolve together, recognizing that knowledge is not a possession to be hoarded but a flowing river that nourishes all who encounter it. Success is redefined, no longer measured by the accumulation of personal wealth or accolades, but by the positive impact one has on the lives of others—the light one brings into the world. Education transcends the narrow goal of survival and becomes a sacred preparation for higher service, aligning each individual not with societal expectations, but with the deeper calling of the soul.

Yet, this vision of Oneness remains distant until we dare to rise beyond self-interest, beyond insecurity, beyond any self-imposed limitations. We must cultivate a generation that seeks not power, but purpose; not dominance, but harmony. For education, at its highest form, should not simply create workers, professionals, or scholars. It should create stewards of wisdom, architects of peace, pioneers of a more enlightened world. And that education begins not in schools, but in the sacred classroom of the home.

The Ultimate Question: What Am I Here to Give?

The destiny of our civilization does not rest solely in the hands of governments, technological marvels, or economic policies. It rests in the awakening consciousness of those who will inherit the earth. If the students of today are to become the enlightened leaders of tomorrow, they must not be taught to ask merely, "How can I succeed?" but rather, "How can I serve?"

Education must cease to be a relentless race to the top and instead become a bridge to something far more enduring—a sacred path that empowers each soul to uplift, to contribute, and to heal. It must rise above the narrow confines of self-centered ambition and embrace the infinite sky of soul-centered contribution. For in the final measure, the worth of education lies not in how much knowledge is amassed, but in how deeply wisdom is embodied; not in how many accolades are earned, but in how many lives are touched; not in how high one ascends, but in how profoundly one understands.

Imagine an education that births not just professionals, but pioneers of transformation. Imagine a world where students are not merely prepared to conform, but to shine—not in rivalry, but in service. Envision schools where the Soul Quotient (SQ)—the ability to lead with wisdom, compassion, and purpose—is held in equal regard to intellectual prowess. In such a world, education would no longer be a ladder to personal gain, but a bridge to sacred purpose. It would teach us not only how to think, but how to feel; not only how to achieve, but how to give. Only then can we cultivate generations who lead with integrity, create with compassion, and co-author a world worthy of our shared humanity.

To embrace this higher vision—to redefine education as the art of adding the highest value—is to awaken the brilliance that already lies dormant in every student. It is to forge a future where knowledge becomes the servant of wisdom, where learning fuels love, and where success is no longer measured by what we accumulate, but by what we offer to the world.

The lifelong, highest-value-adding student is not born—they are sculpted by the hands of self-inquiry, shaped by the fire of awakened learning, and refined through the quiet commitment to serve something greater than themselves. They are the healers, visionaries, innovators, and stewards of a more compassionate and harmonious world. And their journey begins not with the acquisition of knowledge, but with the courage to ask the most sacred of questions: "What am I here to give?"

This is the clarion call. The question is no longer, "Can we rise to meet it?" It is now, "Will we dare to?"

Chapter 21

A Futuristic Transformative Vision of Education

The vision of a reimagined, transformative education finds its most profound expression in the tangible impact of trailblazing models—where pioneers refuse to accept the status quo and instead rise to meet the clarion call of evolution. It is a vision that transcends the mere dissemination of knowledge, reaching instead into the essence of human potential—an education that does not merely prepare students for careers but for a life of purpose, meaning, and conscious service.

One such model is the remarkable case study of Collinwood High School, where a failing system was not rescued by infrastructure or financial intervention, but through the radical awakening of identity and purpose. Another beacon illuminating this path of educational renaissance is the pioneering work of Gurdip Hari, an esteemed educator, philosopher, and author—a man whose vision and commitment to holistic learning mirror my own, making him not merely a collaborator but a twin counterpart in this work, a fellow traveler on the same journey of educational evolution.

Gurdip does not merely reimagine education—he dares to redefine its very essence. To him, learning is not an obligation but a sacred pilgrimage, a journey into the depths of one's potential, a passage that leads not to degrees and titles but to enlightenment and self-mastery. His life's work echoes the very foundation of my own beliefs—that education must not be reduced to mere instruction, but must be an awakening, a revelation, a profound alchemy that transforms not only the mind but the soul.

Education as a Symphony of Wisdom and Innovation

At the heart of this revolution lies a symphony of wisdom, one that integrates timeless, universal truths with contemporary innovation. Gurdip Hari's literary masterpiece, *The Mind is a Labyrinth with Three Keys: Unlock the Secrets of the Conscious, Unconscious and Super-Conscious*, published by Hay House, unveils a profound blueprint for the reawakening of education. He terms this work:

"The Essential Aspects of the Inner Science of our Body, Mind, and Soul—An Integral Component in a School's Curriculum and a Vital Handbook for Parents, Teachers, and Pupils."

More than a book, it is a manifesto, a declaration, a call to revolutionize the way we teach, learn, and cultivate human potential. But he does not merely theorize—he builds. He transforms philosophy into reality, ideas into living, breathing institutions that embody the wisdom he shares.

His vision materializes in the form of Healthy-Mind International School in Accra, Ghana—an educational sanctuary where holistic learning flourishes, where ancient wisdom intertwines seamlessly with modern methodologies, where students are not just trained, but awakened.

He extends an invitation to educators, parents, and visionaries from across the globe to witness this paradigm shift in Ghana—a land steeped in history, affectionately called "The Gold Coast." It is here that one can experience, firsthand, an education system that does not just prepare students for careers but for a life of purpose, meaning, and conscious service.

Education as an Alchemy of Wisdom and Innovation

The sins of modern education, as explored throughout this book, find their ultimate remedy in the living, breathing practices of this innovative school. But more than that, his contributions have not only enhanced my work but have woven a deeper thread of consciousness into its very fabric.

His work does not merely reflect my own beliefs—it expands them. His vision mirrors, strengthens, and elevates the call for transformation that I have long championed. Together, we share the conviction that education must no longer be a mechanical process but an alchemy—a fusion of wisdom, intuition, and mastery, rooted in the spirit of Oneness.

In the corridors of his school, in the souls of the students he nurtures, in the very essence of his mission, I see the manifestation of everything I have sought to express in this book. This is not just an alignment of ideas—it is the convergence of purpose, the meeting of two rivers flowing toward the same boundless ocean of human potential.

This is not just education. This is transformation. At its core, this educational model fosters curiosity rather than suppresses it. It cultivates self-awareness rather than conformity. It encourages self-mastery rather than blind ambition. It integrates service and purpose rather than self-interest.

Mindfulness, creativity, and exploration are not extracurricular luxuries—they are foundational pillars. Through an integrated curriculum encompassing music, arts, sports, yoga, and meditative practices, students are invited to uncover their innate gifts, while simultaneously cultivating resilience, emotional balance, and self-awareness.

This visionary approach does not simply prepare students to excel—it prepares them to evolve. It does not merely train individuals to navigate the world—it empowers them to transform it by mastering their unique talents.

Education Guided by Timeless Wisdom

"Education for the Future, with the Wisdom of the Past."

More than a motto, this guiding principle embodies a revolutionary ethos. It underscores the mission of education to intertwine the richness of ancient traditions with forward-thinking innovation, ensuring that students do not just learn facts, but embody wisdom, resilience, and vision. This philosophy ensures that education is not confined to the mere transmission of knowledge, but becomes a transformative force that shapes character and consciousness. It instills a reverence for diversity, recognizing that wisdom flourishes through the harmonization of varied perspectives. It celebrates cultural interconnectedness, reminding students that they are not isolated individuals but threads in a grand, universal tapestry.

In this reimagined system, students are not merely prepared for economic success—they are cultivated as leaders of consciousness. They are not trained as workers but awakened as visionaries. They are not mass-produced as professionals but ignited as pioneers of change.

At Healthy-Mind International School, students thrive in an environment designed to nurture their entire being—mentally, physically, and spiritually. Daily practices like yoga, inner-science classes, and mindfulness foster self-awareness and emotional intelligence, empowering them to face life's challenges with resilience. Creative outlets in the arts and music foster authentic self-expression, encouraging each student to discover their unique voice. Physical activities and sports build strength, discipline, and teamwork, while meditative and reflective practices forge a lifelong connection to inner stillness and clarity.

The Path to Purpose: The Sacred Triad of Learning

True education cannot be confined within the walls of a school. It flows far beyond, weaving itself into the sacred realms of home and family, where the first and most enduring lessons of life are imparted—not through textbooks, but through the silent eloquence of love, the quiet wisdom of example, and the enduring power of presence.

This is an education that rises beyond rigid structures and conventional teaching, aligning itself with a timeless vision—one that seeks not merely to inform, but to awaken. It is a call for learners, faculty, and parents alike to become lifelong seekers of wisdom, architects of purpose, and masters of their own destinies. It nurtures an infinite vision—a boundless horizon that prepares not just for a career, but for the vast, resplendent possibilities of the soul.

At the heart of this living journey lies The Path to Purpose (PTP) Global Mastership Program—a guiding force in this evolution of learning. Rooted in the understanding that education does not begin in classrooms but in the sacred sanctuary of the home, it highlights the vital collaboration between Pupil, Teacher, and Parent—the divine triad of learning.

Parents are not merely caretakers but co-educators—the first architects of a child's perspective, sculpting their worldview through lessons of compassion, wonder, and character. They are the keepers of wisdom, the nurturers of possibility, and the silent weavers of a child's earliest dreams.

Teachers are not mere instructors but facilitators of revelation—guiding students beyond standardized achievement and into the sovereign expanse of self-discovery, intellectual freedom, and mastery of their innate gifts. They are light-bearers of potential, nurturing not compliance, but consciousness.

Pupils are not passive recipients, but seekers, voyagers, and creators—engaging actively in a purpose-driven education that invites them to rise beyond the limitations of societal expectation and embrace the singular brilliance of their unique design. They are not meant to fit into the world's mold, but to reshape the world itself.

By fostering this sacred triad between Pupil, Teacher, and Parent, education is no longer a mere transaction of knowledge—it becomes a living, breathing force of transformation. It unfolds as an ongoing, immersive odyssey of enlightenment, service, and self-awakening. Anchored in a soulfully woven curriculum, guided by a unique learning framework, dedicated to nurturing each student's unique gifts, this journey invites learners into profound self-realization, global consciousness, and purposeful living. Education ceases to be a race for accumulation—it becomes the gradual blossoming of the soul's radiant light.

It is a path that shapes not only courageous lifelong learners but compassionate leaders—individuals who serve with humility, vision, and heart. Each term, this sacred pilgrimage culminates in a moment of shared celebration, where students rise before their peers, teachers, and families—not to perform, but to offer. Each presentation becomes a living testament: a reflection of their inner and outer evolution, the knowledge they have gathered, the wisdom they have cultivated, and the deeper self they have begun to awaken.

Learning within this holistic sanctuary does not unfold under the weight of pressure, but through the timeless arts of contemplation, exploration, and introspection. Traditional examinations are reserved until the final year, replaced instead by reflective assessments that honor the wholeness of every learner. The goal is not to sort or compare, but to awaken within each soul the sacred power of self-assessment—the ability to chart one's own growth, refine one's own unique path, and align knowledge with a life of meaning, contribution, and higher purpose.

Transformative Tales from the Heartbeat of the School

The stories shared here are drawn from real students, parents, and teachers of Healthy-Mind International School. Their authentic names and journeys have been preserved to honor the truth of their transformation.

Teacher Testimony: The Joy of Teaching Reclaimed

Mrs. Barbara, a teacher of 6 years, confessed that before joining Healthy-Mind School in 2021, she was on the brink of burnout. "Teaching had become mechanical—grading papers, enforcing rules, chasing syllabus deadlines. But here, I rediscovered why I began teaching in the first place. In this space, I am not just an instructor, but a guide, a learner, a witness to transformation. I've seen children blossom not just academically, but emotionally and spiritually. That is the true reward."

Student Awakening: The Boy Who Used to Hate School

Alex once saw school as a place of punishment—a sentence to endure rather than a space to grow. Labeled "difficult" and burdened by attention struggles, he often acted out, not from rebellion, but from frustration and unrecognized potential. That began to shift with the introduction of movement-based learning and immersive explorations into world cultures, nature, and the arts. Slowly, the walls of anxiety began to fall, and something within him stirred.

During a reflective class circle, Alex spoke softly but with clarity: "This school listens to my heart, not just my head—I want to be an astronaut, and my passion is finally being honored." He soon became a vibrant force within the school—joyfully immersed in science, global cultures, and creative exploration. His natural gift for public speaking emerged, and his project presentations became spellbinding, leaving peers and parents captivated by his insight and presence. A boy once reluctant to participate now stood tall as a powerful orator and inspired learner.

Alex's journey was made possible by his father, who moved from Lebanon to Ghana solely to give his son this transformative educational experience at Healthy-Mind. But after three years of financial struggle, he was forced to return home. With tears in his eyes, he said, "There will never be another school like this—it brought joy and purpose into Alex's life, and now we must leave it behind." Though their time at Healthy-Mind came to an early end, the spark it ignited in Alex still burns—a light that will continue to guide him wherever he goes.

A Journey from Self to Service

When Seth first arrived at Healthy-Mind, he carried with him a decade of teaching experience—and a quiet imprint of a system that had taught him to seek personal gain above deeper purpose. Success was measured by what one could acquire, not by what one could offer.

But Healthy-Mind spoke a different language—one that stirred something long dormant within him. Here, education was not a race for rewards, but a path of awakening, rooted in giving, growing, and serving. Slowly, the old mindset gave way to a higher devotion: "How can I contribute?"

Today, nearly five years later, Seth is more than an educator—he is a guide, a seeker, a co-creator of transformation. In this living, breathing community of students, parents, and teachers, he found what true education was always meant to be: not the accumulation of accolades, but the flowering of spirit.

Seth's story reminds us—true education does not merely fill minds; it ignites hearts and elevates souls.

Marvin's Beat: From Silence to Celebration

When Marvin returned to his homeland, Ghana, and joined Healthy-Mind, he arrived quiet and reserved. But behind the shy smile lay a vibrant rhythm—a deep, unspoken passion for drumming. Growing up in Japan, he played in churches and school programs, yet his talent remained largely unrefined—an unpolished gem awaiting purpose, direction, and nurture.

At Healthy-Mind, everything changed. Immersed in a learning environment that valued both intellect and inner passion, Marvin flourished. Music classes opened new dimensions of rhythm and meaning, while subjects like Language & Literature and Humanities sparked a deeper curiosity. "I feel I've grown more here than anywhere else," he shared.

His talent bloomed as he joined the school band and dedicated himself to his craft. At the year-end celebration, Marvin's drumming during "Celebration" by Kool & the Gang mesmerized the audience—joyful, precise, and full of life. In that moment, he was no longer just a student—he was a storyteller, a leader, a radiant beacon of awakened potential.

And his rhythm only continues to rise. With every beat, he drums his way toward new heights, captivating audiences with timeless melodies like "Fly Like an Eagle, Building a Bridge, and The Long Run"—each performance a step deeper into his purpose.

Unwritten Champion

When Kofi first arrived at Healthy-Mind in Year 4, he carried more than just a backpack—he carried a label. A child deemed "dyslexic," a "slow learner," a boy who "couldn't spell." At just nine years old, the world had already placed him inside a narrow box, sealed with quiet judgments.

He struggled with phonics, stumbled over simple spellings, and bore the weary sighs of those who believed he would simply "take time." But we saw something else. We saw a light, flickering beneath frustration—a brilliance not needing correction, but awakening. We listened. We believed. We nurtured.

And slowly, Kofi began to rewrite the story the world had hastily drafted for him. Phonics blossomed into fluency. Spellings became steady, joyful victories. His curiosity—once shackled—found a home where it could unfurl and soar.

Yet his greatest transformation unfolded beyond the classroom—on the tennis court. There, Kofi found his rhythm, his fire. What began as casual lessons turned into fierce devotion. With each swing, each sprint, he shattered the invisible walls once placed around him.

And it didn't end there—in football too, his agility and tactical spark shone bright. Within the sanctuary of the Music Academy, seated humbly behind the drums, he summoned melodies and rhythms with astonishing ease—a glimpse of hidden genius rising, beat by beat, like a song long waiting to be sung.

Today, when Kofi stands before the school community—speaking with clarity, poise, and a confidence once unimaginable—his mother watches from the audience, tears tracing her radiant smile. "Is this the same boy?" she whispers.

Yes. This is Kofi—no longer unwritten.

This is Kofi—unstoppable ever since.

A Parent's Reflection: Education as Healing

Mrs. X, who prefers to remain unnamed, came to Healthy-Mind carrying the quiet ache of a mother's worry. Her daughter—once a lively spirit—had grown muted, burdened by a system that measured worth by numbers and dimmed wonder with constant comparison. "I used to find her crying softly over a single lost mark," she recalled. "Her light was slowly fading."

But at Healthy-Mind, something beautiful began to unfold. Within weeks, the heavy veil of anxiety lifted. Her daughter woke each morning not with dread, but with a spark—eager not to compete, but to discover. "She rushes home now, bursting with stories—not just of math or science, but of empathy, of interconnectedness, of the quiet art of listening."

Here, learning is not a race but a dance—a sacred rhythm of reflection, exploration, and self-realization. Without the crushing weight of high-stakes exams, and guided by projects that nourish purpose rather than pride, her daughter found her own music. She stretched with grace into yoga, danced freely across open spaces, sang with abandon, and grew sturdy in spirit on the sports field.

"Her teachers don't just grade her—they witness her," said Mrs. X, her voice trembling with gratitude. "And now, she too witnesses her own light."

The transformation rippled beyond the school walls. "One evening, as my husband and I stumbled into argument, she quietly placed her small hands in ours and said, 'Can we just pause and breathe together?'" In that simple act, Mrs. X glimpsed a truth deeper than any lesson plan: "This school hasn't just changed her. It has softened our entire home, teaching us all how to live with more grace."

A Teacher's Devotion: Teaching as a Sacred Journey

"I am Courage."

It's not just his name—it's a quiet declaration of how he teaches and lives. When he first encountered Healthy-Mind, he didn't ask about salary or benefits. He offered to serve, even without pay—drawn not by compensation, but by a calling. The school's philosophy awakened something deep within him.

For the past four years, Courage has been more than a teacher. He has been a learner, a guide, and a sculptor of awakened minds. "It's been a profound journey of growth and self-discovery," he shares. "This place constantly calls me to become the best version of myself."

What drew him in was a shared philosophy—one that values understanding over memorization, inquiry over instruction, and purpose over performance. "Healthy-Mind resonates with my soul. It's a space where questions are honored, reflection is nurtured, and every challenge becomes a chance to evolve."

His greatest joy? That glimmer of understanding in a student's eyes—when confusion gives way to clarity, and knowledge becomes lived wisdom. "It's a sacred moment," he says, "when that inner spark catches flame."

In a world where teaching is too often transactional, Courage reminds us that true education is not a job, but a sacred offering—a devotion to the awakening of human potential.

Family Renewal Through Education

Since enrolling their children at Healthy-Mind, one family experienced a quiet but profound transformation—not just in their children, but in the soul of their home. "Our dinner conversations used to revolve around grades, deadlines, and routines," the parents shared. "Now, our children ask us what we were grateful for today, or how we practiced kindness."

The shift was not orchestrated—it was organic, arising from the values gently cultivated at school and echoed at home. The children began leading with curiosity, compassion, and mindfulness, not only in class but around the family table. "It's as if they've become mirrors, reflecting back to us a more thoughtful way of living," they said. "Our children are teaching us how to live better—and for the first time in a long while, we are listening."

A Tale of Two Siblings: Blossoming Beyond Borders

In 2021, siblings Retaj and Zeyad arrived at Healthy-Mind under the diplomatic shadows of their father's posting at the Egyptian Embassy in Ghana. Retaj, just seven years old, entered Year 1 with wide eyes and a heavy heart—unable to speak a word of English, unsure of herself, and feeling adrift in an unfamiliar land. Zeyad, in Year 5, faced similar challenges. Though older, his grasp of English was limited, and he too struggled to find his voice in this new environment.

But something extraordinary unfolded within the nurturing embrace of Healthy-Mind. Through its soul-centered curriculum, compassionate guidance, and immersive programs that honored both language and spirit, the siblings slowly began to transform.

For Retaj, it was a metamorphosis. What began in quiet hesitation soon gave way to curiosity, and then to courage. By Year 3, the once-silent girl who felt invisible in a foreign tongue stood tall as a beacon of confidence and eloquence. Her speeches, delivered with grace and conviction, echoed through school halls. She had blossomed into an orator of exceptional talent—her voice not only fluent but full of fire, inspiring peers and teachers alike. And as if her words weren't powerful enough, she found yet another language in movement—ballet. With poise and discipline, Retaj became a standout performer, her expressive performances weaving stories without words. On stage, she danced not only with precision but with soul, captivating audiences and revealing a newfound artistry within.

Zeyad too found his wings. In the creative classrooms and reflective spaces of Healthy-Mind, his potential unfolded like the petals of a long-awaited bloom. His quiet strength, sharp intellect, and growing confidence marked him as a leader in the making—a young mind with the vision and character to one day guide his nation. His teachers often whispered, "There's a statesman in this boy."

When their father's tenure at the embassy came to an end in 2024, he tried with all his might to extend their stay, knowing what this school had done for his children. But duty called him home. As he prepared to leave, his eyes welled with pride and longing. "Why can't we have schools like Healthy-Mind in Egypt?" he asked. "Why not across the world?"

The question remains—not as a lament, but as a challenge to the world: to reimagine education not as a system of survival, but as a sanctuary where every child, like Retaj and Zeyad, can rise into the fullness of who they are meant to become.

The Voice Within

When Sandra first walked through the gates of Healthy-Mind, she was like a delicate bud—shy, playful, quietly observant. Having transferred from another school, she wore a gentle smile, yet her eyes spoke of hesitation—as if holding a secret she herself had yet to discover.

We noticed her sweetness, her occasional giggles during lessons, her quiet confidence in the water as a graceful swimmer—but beyond that, she remained a tender mystery waiting to unfold. Weeks melted into months, and slowly, Sandra began to bloom.

Her academic clarity sharpened, her focus deepened—each day revealing a newer, more luminous version of herself. Yet her true turning point came unannounced, like a gift hidden in plain sight. It happened during a music class.

As the piano keys softly awakened the room, Sandra—almost by accident—began to hum. What followed silenced every corner of the hall. Her voice—crystal clear, achingly pure—rose into the air with effortless beauty, wrapping the room in wonder. The music facilitator, stunned mid-note, could only listen. We captured a small recording and sent it to her mother.

The response was unforgettable. There was a long pause, then the quiet sound of tears over the phone. "I didn't even know my daughter could sing," her mother whispered, her voice trembling. "Not like this."

At Healthy-Mind, this is the magic we hold sacred: We do not merely teach—we uncover.

We do not merely instruct—we listen for the voice within. Sandra was not just found. She was finally heard.

A Call to Action: Education for Generations to Come

These stories are not isolated miracles—they are proof of what becomes possible when we allow education to return to its sacred roots. When students are seen not as products but as possibilities, when teachers reclaim their role as nurturers of potential, and when families are welcomed into the circle of growth, transformation becomes inevitable.

This vision redefines education as more than a system of instruction—it is a sacred pilgrimage, a journey not merely of acquiring knowledge but of self-discovery, purpose, and global contribution. It is an odyssey that transcends the confines of textbooks and classrooms, one that nourishes the mind, strengthens the body, and awakens the spirit. It is a path that does not merely produce scholars but forges architects of a compassionate world, leaders sculpted by integrity, visionaries imbued with wisdom.

Yet, this revolution does not begin with institutions or policies. It begins in the silent chambers of the soul—in the minds of those who dare to ask a different question. Not "What's in it for me?" but "What am I here to give?"

This is the ultimate question—the question that transformed my own life and redefined the trajectory of my company, POLYCARB, from the brink of collapse into a beacon of success and prosperity. It was not a shift in strategy that saved us but a shift in consciousness—a surrender to the higher principle of Oneness, a realization that the greatest measure of success is not in what we accumulate, but in what we contribute.

This very question guided Gurdip Hari through his own trials, through his own moments of reckoning, shaping his rise to success. It is no coincidence that our paths have converged in this work. Though we were not born of the same blood, nor raised in the same place, our spirits were forged in the same eternal flame. We are brothers in purpose, twin architects bound not by lineage, but by a shared devotion to Oneness, service, and purpose.

We hold the same unshakable belief that education is not merely about acquiring knowledge—it is about awakening wisdom. The true essence of education is not to give a child what they do not need, but to awaken what they already possess—to nurture their divine uniqueness, to refine their inherent gifts, and to shape them into masters of their own purpose, so they may serve the world in their highest capacity.

This is the moment where education ceases to be a mere institution and becomes a movement. A movement of transformation. A movement of higher purpose. A movement that ignites the boundless potential of our inner unity within every student, every teacher, every parent.

Thus, we do not merely change education—we reshape the future. We do not merely improve the system—we awaken humanity itself.

Chapter 22

Coming Full Circle

This final chapter marks not merely the end of a book, but the completion of a journey—a return to the beginning, now seen with awakened eyes. We began by unearthing the deepest flaws and "sins" of modern education: its alliance with insecurity, its glorification of conformity, and its abandonment of purpose. From the erosion of curiosity and creativity to the mechanization of learning, we explored how education has strayed from its sacred potential.

We then ventured into the transformative power of self-knowledge, emotional intelligence, communication, and service, revealing how a new model of learning—one rooted in wisdom, Oneness, and contribution—can uplift not only individuals but the very fabric of society. With visionary blueprints and real-life case studies, we have witnessed what becomes possible when education reclaims its soul.

And now, we complete the circle by returning to the origin of all true education—the sacred question that reawakens purpose: "What am I here to give?"

A Revolutionary Shift: From Conformity to Purpose

At the heart of this transformation lies a radical reimagining of education's purpose. No longer can we allow schooling to remain a rigid structure centered on memorization, standardized metrics, and career preparation. Instead, it must become a sacred invitation—a call for each student to discover the truth of who they are and what they are uniquely here to give.

This shift demands an educational paradigm that transcends conformity and empowers students to uncover their own path.

It must celebrate individuality, honoring the truth that every soul carries an original spark meant to uplift the world. It must foster inner confidence, nurturing the understanding that one's worth is not tied to accolades or approval, but to the authenticity of one's presence. It must instill a deep sense of service, guiding learners to align their lives not with superficial ambition, but with meaningful contribution. And it must redefine success—not as wealth or fame, but as the depth of one's impact, the lives one touches, and the legacy of love one leaves behind.

This is the revolution we are called to embrace—a bold departure from conformity, and a sovereign journey into purpose.

The Pillars of Transformational Education

Throughout this book, we have explored key principles that form the backbone of a reimagined education system. These pillars include:

1.   Self-Knowledge as the Foundation

- Who they are—Beyond labels and achievements, they must connect with the universal energy that animates all life.
- How they are designed—Understanding their strengths, challenges, and limitless inner potential.
- What they are here to give—Aligning their education with a higher purpose rooted in service and contribution, through the discovery and cultivation of their innate gifts.

This self-knowledge cultivates resilience, creativity, and empathy—qualities that allow students to navigate life's complexities with clarity and confidence.

2.   Curiosity-Driven Learning

Education must break free from the chains of mere memorization and standardized testing and instead ignite the flame of curiosity. This can be achieved through:

- Inquiry-based learning—Encouraging students to ask profound questions and seek their own answers.
- Experiential education—Integrating real-world projects, mentorship, and service learning.
- Interdisciplinary connections—Blending science, philosophy, creativity, and ethics to present knowledge as a holistic symphony rather than isolated subjects.

When curiosity replaces compliance, learning ceases to be an obligation and becomes a lifelong passion.

3. Values-Centered Education

Education must not only sharpen intellect but also cultivate character. It must inspire:

- Integrity and ethical discernment—Guiding students to make decisions that honor both self and society.
- Service-based learning—Rooting education in acts of kindness and contribution.
- Teachers and Parents as role models—Mentors who live by example, not just by instruction.

A student who masters knowledge but lacks values is a student half-educated.

4. Fostering Emotional and Social Intelligence

In a world where technical skills are easily automated, human connection remains irreplaceable. Schools must prioritize emotional intelligence by:

- Teaching emotional literacy—Helping students understand, express, and regulate their emotions.
- Encouraging collaboration—Fostering environments where students learn the power of unity over division.

- Creating safe spaces—Where students feel heard, valued, and empowered to express their truth.

For in the absence of emotional intelligence, no amount of intellect can build a just and harmonious world.

5.   Integrating Purpose and Service

Education must transcend individual success and guide students toward a vision greater than themselves by:

- Reframing education as a service—Not "What's in it for me?" but "What am I here to give?"
- Teaching interconnectedness—Helping students see that their actions ripple across humanity.
- Encouraging purpose-driven projects—Where students apply their learning to solve real-world challenges.

For true fulfillment is not found in self-interest but in selfless service.

The Core Operating Thread: ONENESS

As emphasized in previous chapters, Oneness is not merely a philosophy—it is the eternal thread that binds the fabric of existence. It is the divine rhythm that pulses through all of creation, the silent symphony in which every soul plays its part. It is the recognition that we are not separate entities struggling in isolation but interconnected expressions of the same universal breath.

Education, at its highest calling, must embody this principle. It must cease to be an instrument of division and become a sacred bridge—one that unites minds, heals hearts, and awakens souls to the profound truth that we are all part of an indivisible whole. Without this paradigm, education will remain a fragmented endeavor, reinforcing the illusion of separateness, fostering competition over collaboration, and perpetuating the struggles that plague our world.

To embrace this timeless truth within education is to reimagine learning as a journey not toward personal achievement alone, but toward collective elevation. It is to see knowledge not as a means to power but as a pathway to wisdom. It is to understand that the highest purpose of education is not the accumulation of facts but the illumination of consciousness.

The Call for a Paradigm Shift

When we consider the title of a June 5, 2023, Newsweek article, "Is a Paradigm Shift Needed for School Learning?" the answer is a resounding YES!

Education can no longer remain confined within the walls of institutions, reduced to an accumulation of grades and credentials. A true education is a whole-life proposition—one that extends beyond textbooks and classrooms, reaching into the deepest chambers of our being and radiating outward to touch every life we encounter. It must infuse our existence with creativity, compassion, and an unwavering commitment to the betterment of all.

The responsibility for this transformation does not rest on schools alone. It is a calling for all of us—to become lifelong learners, to uplift one another, and to rise together into higher states of consciousness. It demands that we transcend the shackles of fear, insecurity, greed, and ego—the forces that have kept humanity trapped in cycles of suffering and limitation. Until we make the conscious choice to free ourselves from these chains, we will remain bound to a treadmill existence, mistaking motion for progress while moving nowhere at all.

The Flourishing Human Spirit

For too long, modern education has mirrored the rigid mechanics of an industrial assembly line—a system obsessed with efficiency, uniformity, and standardized outcomes. Students are batched, measured, and evaluated not for their uniqueness, but for their ability to conform to predetermined molds. Creativity is overshadowed by compliance, curiosity is dulled by routine, and the boundless potential of the human spirit is shackled by rigid frameworks designed for mere survival, not for thriving.

But true learning does not belong to factories; it belongs to gardens. Growth cannot be coerced—it must be nurtured. Just as a farmer does not dictate how each seed will sprout but instead cultivates the right conditions for it to flourish, so too must education shift from an industrialized model to one rooted in nature's wisdom. Each learner is unique, unfolding in their own time, in their own way, when nourished by the right environment.

And what is the most fertile ground for this flourishing? It is the infinite thread that binds us all…

This is the fundamental realization that we are not separate, competing entities, but interconnected beings woven into the grand fabric of existence. It is the recognition that education is not just about personal success, but about adding the highest value in every thought, word, and action—for all of humanity, for all beings, and for the planet itself.

When this principle becomes the heartbeat of education, we no longer mass-produce minds that conform; we cultivate souls that flourish, innovate, and serve. This is the essence of a Complete & Transformative Education—one that does not merely equip students for careers but awakens them to their purpose. It is the kind of education that does not just teach knowledge but instills wisdom. It does not just create professionals—it creates pioneers, visionaries, and custodians of a better world.

This is how we move beyond being mere inhabitants of the world and evolve into true human beings—not defined by what we take, but by what we give.

The Missing Principle in Our Progress

Despite our loftiest achievements—our Nobel laureates and towering intellects, our technological marvels that stretch beyond the stars, our sprawling economic empires, and the most sophisticated political systems ever conceived...

Despite world-class healthcare, breathtaking industrial advancements, and the dawn of artificial intelligence that now dares to rival human cognition...

Despite all of this—we remain adrift in a tempest of chaos, division, and unrest. For no matter how many structures we build, how many fortunes we amass, or how many frontiers we conquer, the world will continue to fracture, to hunger, and to wage war within itself...

Until the truth of Oneness is no longer a concept we admire, but a reality we embody. Until it is woven into the fabric of every thought, every word, and every deed. Until it is lived not as an abstract philosophy, but as an unshakable presence—the breath that animates our being, the ground upon which we stand, and the sacred rhythm by which we move through the world.

This is not a poetic aspiration. It is the imperative of our survival— the immutable truth that humanity, the Earth, and all sentient life are not separate threads—but celestial strands of a single, divine tapestry, intricately interwoven and bound by a shared destiny.

Until we awaken to this truth, we will remain captives of illusion—imprisoned by artificial borders of race, nation, religion, and ideology. We will continue to mistake separation for strength, conflict for progress, and domination for power.

But when we begin to live from the cosmic truth of our divine origin—when unity becomes the very foundation of our existence— we will cease to be adversaries and rise as co-creators. We will move beyond limitation, unlocking the boundless potential of humanity. We will transcend the war within and the war with one another. And we will reclaim the ancient harmony that was never truly lost—only forgotten.

In that remembrance, we will no longer merely imagine a better world.

We will become it.

The Question That Changes Everything

The education envisioned in these pages is not merely a reform of curriculum, nor simply an intellectual endeavor—it is a sacred summons to awaken. It is a call for educators to rise as illuminators of potential, for parents to embrace their role as the first teachers and bearers of generational wisdom, and for students to become seekers of truth and sculptors of a new reality. And for leaders, visionaries, and changemakers to dismantle the crumbling scaffolds of conformity and co-create an education that breathes with purpose, curiosity, compassion, and conscious design.

But know this: the great transformation does not begin in institutions—it begins in you. In the quiet sanctuary of your own heart. In the questions you dare to whisper. In the choices you make when no one is watching. In the love you offer without applause or reward. It begins in the courage to unlearn, to dissolve the inherited illusions of separation, and to rise beyond the shadows of fear, self-importance, and division—into the vastness of unity, clarity, and truth.

It begins the moment you pause long enough to ask yourself the most sacred and transformative question of all:

"What am I here to give?"

For within that question lies the seed of all true learning—not to acquire, but to awaken; not to rise alone, but to lift the world with you.

A Closing Note of Mystical Significance: The Number 22

The number **22** is often called the Master Builder—the vibration of divine architecture. In numerology and mystic philosophy, it represents the union of the spiritual and material, the capacity to dream and the power to build. It is not only the number of vision, but of practical realization. It bridges heaven and earth.

That this book concludes on Chapter **22** is not accidental—it is alchemical. For this work is not only a critique but a creation. Not merely a diagnosis, but a design. It calls forth not just reformers, but rebuilders. It invites each reader to rise as a Master Builder of a new world—where education is not a ladder to climb, but a circle to complete; not a commodity, but a sacred act of remembering who we are, and what we are here to give.

This book is a beacon—for schools, for seekers, for societies—who long to rise beyond the ruins of separation and reclaim the harmony of a more enlightened humanity. May its message live on—not only in systems, but in souls. Not only in policies, but in practice. Not only in minds, but in movements.

And may every child, every teacher, every parent who holds this vision—become the builders of a new dawn.

May it be so.

Invocation of 22

A Benediction for the Builders of Global Educational Reform

O Flame of Twenty-Two, Master Architect of Awakening,
Guide of those who rise to restore, to realign, to rebuild.
Let every word scribed in these pages echo through the halls of time,
A call to re-enchant the world through education born of the soul.

May unity be our cornerstone,
And compassion our compass.
Let each school become a sanctuary,
Each lesson a light,
Each child a vessel of vast and untold potential.

Let our purpose no longer be to compete,
But to contribute.
Not to dominate, but to uplift.
Not to survive, but to serve.

O sacred number, you who carry the code of mastery and manifestation,
May this, the 22nd chapter, mark the turning of a greater wheel.
A revolution not of rebellion, but of remembrance.
Not of force, but of vision.

And through this offering—this book, this blueprint, this prayer,
May we begin again.
Not with answers, but with deeper questions.
Not with finality, but with faith.

Faith in what education can become.
Faith in what humanity is destined to be.
Faith in the sacred path of becoming,
And in the grace of returning.

Returning full circle,
To a world restored.
To children reawakened.
To learning reborn.
Where education is no longer a system,
But a soul in motion.

And so, let this book not close, but open,
A gateway, a summons, a gentle awakening across the world.
May its words ripple into classrooms and conversations,
Into villages and cities, into policies and prayers.

Let this be our turning point,
Where learning becomes love in action,
And where every child, every teacher, every parent,
Rises as a builder of a more luminous tomorrow.

And as the circle completes,
A new world of true education begins…

Invitation to the Sacred Blueprint

Beneath the visible chapters of this book lies an invisible current,
a sacred blueprint woven through symbols, scriptures, and stars.

This journey was never linear.
It moved like breath, like music, like the soul's own remembering,
spiraling through archetypes of the Tarot,
ascending the pathways of Kabbalah's Tree of Life,
echoing Krishna's wisdom beneath the din of battle,
and flowing with the divine current of Oneness, as revealed by Guru
Nanak.

What began not as a critique, but as a transformation,
now spirals toward its inner axis,
where all teachings converge, all seekers meet,
and all learning becomes remembrance.

What follows is not a conclusion,
but a return to origin through deeper pattern.
Step now into the architecture behind the story,
the silent symphony beneath every word you've read.

Appendix: The Mystical Journey of the Soul— Tarot, Kabbalah, the Wisdom of Krishna and Guru Nanak in The Sins of Education

Beyond the chapters lie the constellations that shaped them—hidden patterns, ancient wisdoms, and eternal truths woven through the soul's journey across time and tradition...

Throughout this work, *The Sins of Education* has quietly followed an ancient map—an invisible but sacred architecture drawn from the Fool's Journey of the Tarot's Major Arcana, the mystical ascent of consciousness through the Kabbalistic Tree of Life, the timeless teachings of Krishna to Arjuna upon the battlefield of Kurukshetra, and Guru Nanak's celestial revelation of Oneness flowing through the sacred hymns of divine remembrance.

Though these sacred traditions emerged across different continents and ages, they reveal one universal truth: The soul's path is not linear, but spiral—a journey from confusion to wisdom, from division to unity, from self-preservation to selfless service.

The Fool stands at the precipice of life, innocent and untethered; Arjuna stands upon the Chariot, overwhelmed by doubt and duty; The seeker ascends the Tree of Life, passing through the gates of knowledge, surrender, mastery. And the Sikh—the eternal learner—walks the path of divine remembrance, awakening to the truth of Ik Onkar: the sacred Oneness pulsing through all of creation.

In the unfolding of this book, each chapter mirrors one sacred stage in the soul's pilgrimage—toward awakening, toward mastery, and toward the eternal harmony that underlies all creation. This mystical journey is not merely theoretical; it reflects the ageless path of every soul across every tradition: to learn, to unlearn, to serve, to transform, and ultimately—to return Home.

Below, you will find the deeper correspondence between:
Each Tarot archetype,
Each chapter of this book,
Each great lesson from Krishna to Arjuna in the Bhagavad Gita,
And each divine revelation from Guru Nanak's sacred teachings.

Together, they weave an eternal tapestry of sacred education—where the mystic, the seeker, the warrior, and the student are ultimately revealed to be one.

The Fool's Journey Through The Sins of Education

Card 0. The Fool

Chapter 0: Introduction: A Mind is a Terrible Thing to Waste

The Fool symbolizes both the beginning and the end—the sacred zero, the number of infinity, the endless spiral of learning, unlearning, and becoming.

At the threshold of education's corrupted promises, the Fool steps forward, arms wide open to the unknown, bearing the innocence that believes learning will lead to liberation. With the sun behind him, and a song of possibility within, this first naive step is essential—without it, the journey of awakening could never begin.

This chapter captures the soul at the brink: filled with radiant hope, yet unaware of the illusions that lie ahead. Education, once meant to be a bridge to liberation, has become a gilded cage, confining rather than freeing. Yet even within this broken architecture, the first breath of transformation begins—not with mastery, but with contemplation, exploration, and introspection.

The Fool stands as the one who dares to contemplate the purpose of his own journey, who sets out to explore the terrain of existence beyond what has been taught, and who, in silent moments, begins the deep work of introspection—asking not only what to learn, but who is the one learning?

Sacred Parallel – The Fool and Krishna's First Encounter with Arjuna

The Fool steps into the unknown, led by curiosity and pure potential, unaware of the trials that await. So too does Arjuna, trembling upon his chariot at the dawn of battle, paralyzed by doubt and despair.

Both represent the soul before awakening—sincere yet scattered, hopeful yet lost, torn between uncertainty and purpose.

As Krishna begins to guide Arjuna back to his sacred purpose, we witness the very first light of inner remembrance—a soul called not to escape life's battlefield, but to enter it with courage, wisdom, and divine alignment. The battlefield becomes not merely a war of arrows, but a sacred space for introspection, contemplation, and ultimately, exploration of dharma, action, and surrender.

Sacred Parallel – The Fool and Guru Nanak's Vision of the Eternal Seeker

Guru Nanak begins the revelations with the primordial question: "Sochai soch na hova-ee je soch-ee lakh vaar"—One cannot become pure by thought alone, even if one contemplates hundreds of thousands of times.

Like the Fool, Guru Nanak speaks to the humble beginning of the seeker's path—a step not grounded in intellectual mastery, but in surrender, trust, and divine remembrance. Every Sikh, he reminds us, is a lifelong learner—an eternal seeker walking the path of humility, awareness, and alignment with the divine order.

This first revelation dismantles the illusion that contemplation alone is enough—that purity, truth, or liberation can be attained through thought in isolation. Instead, it calls the seeker to move beyond the mind—into exploration of the living Word, and deep introspection into one's alignment with the divine command of Ik Onkaar: Oneness in motion.

The Fool's journey echoes this timeless call: Begin not with the arrogance of knowledge, but with the innocence of wonder. This is not ignorance—it is the sacred readiness to be transformed by the Unknown.

Card 1. The Magician
Chapter 1: Why Learning is Such a Hassle

The Magician is the master of manifestation and represents untapped potential within every soul, wielding the four elemental tools—thought, emotion, will, and spirit.

This chapter shows how modern education stifles these tools, reducing curiosity to compliance. It calls students to reclaim their sacred instruments and remember that true learning is alchemy—the conscious weaving of ideas, dreams, and action into the manifestation of a meaningful, vibrant life, transforming potential into power.

Sacred Parallel – The Magician and Krishna's Call to Inner Power

The Magician stands at the threshold of creation, wielding the sacred tools of mind, heart, will, and intention—a master in potential, yet unaware of how his powers have been buried beneath systems of control.

Krishna reminds Arjuna that he too possesses divine instruments—intellect, discipline, memory, and purpose—but they must be reclaimed from illusion and confusion. Just as the Magician must remember his essence, Krishna calls Arjuna to awaken his spiritual force and rise beyond limitation.True power begins with the recognition that we are already equipped to fulfill our sacred calling—if only we dare to remember.

In education, this means empowering each learner to reclaim their inner tools—not merely to pass exams, but to manifest vision into reality, to cultivate soul-driven agency, and to realize that true power lies in conscious, purposeful creation.

Sacred Parallel – The Magician and Guru Nanak's Call to Inner Activation

Guru Nanak declares: "Pawan guru, pani pita, mata dharat mahat."— Air is the Guru, Water the Father, and Earth the Great Mother.

In these elemental invocations, Guru Nanak reveals that creation itself is a living scripture—each force, each element, a sacred teacher. This mirrors the Magician's table, where the tools of transformation—thought, emotion, will, and spirit—already await the soul's awakening.

Where Krishna calls Arjuna to reclaim his inner strength, Guru Nanak beckons the seeker to recognize the divine already imprinted in all of existence. Like the Magician, each of us holds latent power—not to dominate, but to align; not to possess, but to serve.

True magic, then, is not illusion—it is remembrance. It is the conscious activation of our sacred instruments in harmony with the cosmic song.

To truly educate is to awaken—not to suppress the learner's innate gifts, but to activate them in harmony with life's deeper rhythm. Learning should become a sacred apprenticeship in becoming: cultivating clarity of thought, courage of will, tenderness of emotion, stillness of spirit, and the quiet strength of inner sovereignty. In this way, each student is not trained to conquer the world, but empowered to co-create with it—as a vessel of purpose and awakened power.

Card 2. The High Priestess
Chapter 2: The Formation of Our Core Character

The High Priestess is the guardian of unseen realms—the keeper of subconscious mysteries and soul-blueprints yet to be revealed.

Here, the soul first encounters the hidden forces—emotional, ancestral, and societal—that mold character long before intellect can bloom. This chapter unveils the veiled architecture of epigenetics, early conditioning, and inherited traits, revealing that true education must not merely inform the mind, but reach into the innermost sanctum of the self—where destiny is quietly seeded, waiting to awaken.

Sacred Parallel – The High Priestess and Krishna's Revelation of the Hidden Self

The High Priestess sits between the pillars of mystery and memory, guarding the threshold to the inner sanctum—where dreams stir, ancestral echoes linger, and the quiet scripts of the subconscious shape the visible stage of life. Her silence speaks not of absence, but of presence too profound for ordinary words.

Krishna, in his divine counsel to Arjuna, lifts this very veil—revealing that the true Self is neither the body nor the conditioned mind, but the eternal soul beyond time. In both teachings, the call is clear: one must look inward to understand outward action. For until the inner world is illumined, the outer world remains a reflection of illusion.

Education, therefore, must become a sacred mirror—reflecting not merely the world, but the soul within. It must guide students through the subtle terrain of their inner life, helping them discern the hidden imprints that color perception and shape destiny. Only when the inner eye awakens can the outer life become a conscious expression of truth.

Sacred Parallel – The High Priestess and Guru Nanak's Unveiling of the Inner Self

Guru Nanak proclaims: "Thapiaa na jaa-ay keetaa na ho-ay, aapey aap niranjan so-ay."—The Divine cannot be constructed nor imposed; He is immaculate, self-radiant, and ever-existent.

Like the High Priestess, who holds the keys to the sacred interior, Nanak summons the seeker to turn inward—to pierce the veils of illusion and remember the soul's radiant source, hidden beneath layers of fear, conditioning, and inherited belief. The true self is not discovered in rituals, dogma, or the gaze of the world, but in the hush of inner silence, the stillness of meditation, and alignment with divine law.

In this light, education must unfold as a sacred unveiling—not the mere accumulation of knowledge, but a quiet revelation that helps students reclaim their original brilliance, their divine genesis, and the boundless potential seeded in the sanctuary of the soul.

Card 3. The Empress
Chapter 3: It's More than Just Biology

The Empress embodies creation, abundance, and the nurturing womb of life.

Education, in its highest form, must become a sacred garden where emotional safety and human dignity are tenderly cultivated. Only within this fertile soil can a child's innate confidence and creative potential blossom into fullness.This chapter reveals the path from the shadows of insecurity and survivalism toward the glorious act of becoming—where the student ceases to merely adapt, and instead rises as an architect of destiny.

Sacred Parallel – The Empress and Krishna's Vision of Nurturing the World

The Empress is the sacred mother—the one who nourishes life not only with love, but with wisdom that protects and empowers.

Krishna speaks of Prakriti, the divine feminine energy—as the womb of all existence, the matrix through which the entire cosmos is conceived, sustained, and transformed. He reveals to Arjuna that this creative force is not passive; it is active intelligence, the sacred rhythm of nature itself. And from this sacred ground arise not only beauty and nourishment, but also the courage to embody righteousness through compassion, and the clarity to follow the path of truth with unwavering grace.

True education must mirror this divine motherhood—not merely filling minds with knowledge, but nurturing the whole being. It must cultivate the soil of the soul, where confidence grows alongside compassion, and reverence for life becomes the very root from which wisdom flowers.

Sacred Parallel – The Empress and Guru Nanak's Celebration of the Divine Feminine

Guru Nanak sings: "So kyon manda aakhiye jit jammeh raajan."— Why call her inferior, from whom kings are born?

With these timeless words, Guru Nanak exalts the feminine as the primal force of creation—the sacred womb from which life, love, and lineage emerge. Just as The Empress embodies fertility, compassion, and soulful abundance, Nanak reminds us that the mother is not merely a nurturer of bodies, but a bearer of worlds, deserving of reverence beyond measure.

In both The Empress and Nanak's divine insight, we are called to restore dignity, love, and sacredness to all acts of nurturing. For without honoring the feminine—within and around us—no true wisdom can blossom, and no soul can fully thrive.

Creation, then, is not a conquest—it is a communion. And education, at its highest, becomes a sacred act of mothering the soul—nurturing the divine spark within each child with patience, presence, and reverence. For in every student lies a world waiting to be born, and it is through love, not control, that true learning takes root and flourishes.

Card 4. The Emperor

Chapter 4: Living Our Knowledge vs Living Our Habits

The Emperor establishes sacred order, conscious authority, and the architecture of sovereignty.

Here, the veil is lifted to show how true education must forge sovereign beings—rulers of their own inner kingdoms—not mechanical creatures trapped in inherited routines. This chapter insists that authentic learning demands conscious governance of self, not blind allegiance to obsolete scripts, societal patterns, or unconscious habits long past their relevance.

Sacred Parallel – The Emperor and Krishna's Call to Inner Sovereignty

The Emperor represents structure, discipline, and rightful authority—not as control over others, but as mastery of one's own inner kingdom.

Krishna urges Arjuna to rise above habitual thinking, to govern not from inherited roles or reactive emotion, but from soul-guided responsibility. Just as the Emperor must build his rule on inner law rather than external command, Arjuna is called to shift from blind action to awakened governance.

True leadership begins when knowledge becomes embodiment, and habits yield to conscious direction.

Education, therefore, must cultivate this inner sovereignty—empowering students to lead not by imitation, but through self-mastery. It must train minds to think independently, hearts to act compassionately, and spirits to rise in allegiance to truth rather than the chains of dogma.

Sacred Parallel – The Emperor and Guru Nanak's Vision of Sovereign Living

Guru Nanak says: "Man jeetai jag jeet."—One who conquers the mind, conquers the world.

This timeless truth echoes the essence of the Emperor. Sovereignty, Nanak reminds us, is not granted by title or power—it is born from the mastery of one's own inner terrain. He who transcends ego, aligns with divine order, and governs his mind with wisdom, becomes the true emperor—unshaken, purposeful, and free.

The Emperor, too, is not a tyrant, but a steward—upholding sacred order not through force, but through inner clarity and just action. In this light, education must become a throne of self-governance, teaching students to rise as sovereign beings—not by ruling others, but by ruling themselves.

Thus, Guru Nanak's vision, Krishna's wisdom, and the Emperor's archetype all converge to teach us: the greatest kingdom we can ever rule is our own consciousness, and the purpose of education is to help every student ascend that throne with dignity, wisdom, and sacred will.

Card 5. The Hierophant
Chapter 5: The Power of Change

The Hierophant stands as the sacred bridge between heaven and earth—a bearer of timeless truth and initiator of evolving consciousness.

In this chapter, rigid traditions are challenged, and students are called into dynamic models of learning that honor both ancient wisdom and the living force of evolution. True education becomes not the memorization of doctrines, but an initiation into continuous seeking of life's higher mysteries—anchored in purpose, propelled by the fire of conscious change, and liberated from the mere conformity to fading forms.

Sacred Parallel – The Hierophant and Krishna as the Divine Teacher

The Keeper of Living Wisdom bridges heaven and earth—guardian of sacred traditions and revealer of eternal truths.

In Krishna, we meet the ultimate Guru—one who does not cling to static doctrine, but breathes life into spiritual wisdom through living relevance. As Krishna redefines Arjuna's understanding of success, sacrifice, and duty, he becomes the true Hierophant: not a keeper of dogma, but a liberator of consciousness.

Education, too, must blossom from frozen instruction to sacred initiation—guiding students not toward conformity, but toward transformation. It must move beyond passive absorption into active engagement—where the teacher is not merely a source of answers, but a catalyst of awakening.

Sacred Parallel – The Hierophant and Guru Nanak's Teaching of Living Wisdom

Guru Nanak declared: "Aape beej aape hee khaahu." Each human being harvests what they cultivate—wisdom grows through conscious action.

And yet, he gently reminded the seeker that the Divine does not reside in pages alone. True wisdom, he taught, is not confined to ritual or rote—it is awakened in the living pulse of daily life, in the stillness of meditation, in the breath of compassion, in the divine spark shimmering within every soul.

Like the Hierophant, Guru Nanak stands between the visible and the invisible—not as a gatekeeper of doctrine, but as a revealer of inner light. The Guru is not a position of hierarchy, but a state of consciousness—one that awakens the seeker to the divine resonance within themselves.

Thus, education must evolve from static tradition into sacred dialogue—a living communion with Truth that flows through word, action, silence, and wonder. In the presence of such wisdom, learning becomes not the memorization of holiness, but the radiant expression of it—where the classroom becomes a sanctuary, and every lesson a doorway to divine realization.

Card 6. The Lovers
Chapter 6: Who or What Guides Our Education System?

The Lovers signify sacred choice—the inner union of heart and mind aligned with divine values.

Education, like the Lovers standing at the crossroads, faces a profound choice: Will it serve the energies of fear, control, and fragmentation—or awaken to the pathways of freedom, authenticity, and love? This chapter urges a return to soul-centered choice as the living foundation of all learning systems. It reveals that the future of education—and indeed of humanity—hinges upon which path we choose: one of self-interest that deepens division, or one that leads toward wholeness, unity, and liberation.

Sacred Parallel – The Lovers and Arjuna's Sacred Choice

The Lovers represent the great inner decision: to remain in fragmented duality or to align with divine love and higher purpose.

Arjuna stands upon the precipice of battle—not merely a war of kingdoms, but a war within. He is torn between loyalty to blood and loyalty to duty, between the familiar bonds of family and the call of his soul's deeper truth. It is here, in the trembling silence of his inner conflict, that Krishna becomes not just a charioteer, but the voice of the Eternal—reminding him that the sacred choice is not between good and bad, but between illusion and truth, fear and faith, comfort and purpose.

Like the Lovers standing at the crossroads, education systems too must choose: will we preserve systems rooted in division and control, or will we rise to nurture freedom, wholeness, and inner alignment—guiding each learner to choose love not as emotion, but as their way of being?

Sacred Parallel – The Lovers and Guru Nanak's Revelation of Divine Union

Guru Nanak declared: "Ik Onkar"—There is but One Creator, woven into the fabric of all that lives. This primal utterance does not merely affirm unity—it dissolves the illusion of separation and unveils the divine current pulsing through every being, every breath, every bond.

To walk the path of love, he taught, is to move beyond ego, beyond judgment, beyond the false walls that divide. The true Lover is one who sees no "other," who chooses union over separation, compassion over indifference, and humility over pride.

In the Lovers' sacred archetype, this revelation finds reflection: each soul stands at a crossroads—to remain entranced by illusion, or to awaken into divine remembrance, where love is no longer a fleeting emotion, but a resplendent state of being.

Education, too, must be rooted in this sacred consciousness—not merely instructing minds, but guiding hearts to live as one, to serve in love, and to recognize the divine beloved in all.

Card 7. The Chariot

Chapter 7: My Journey through the Two Paths of Education

The Chariot symbolizes mastery of dual forces—the triumph of spirit over division, and the journey forward, not through brute force, but through inner alignment.Traditionally, the Chariot is drawn by two opposing sphinxes or horses—one black, one white—representing the positive and negative forces that perpetually pull the soul in opposite directions.

True victory for the Charioteer is not found in conquering or suppressing either side, but in holding the sacred tension between opposites and discovering the path of integration—the middle way.

This chapter embodies that sacred trial. Riding the Chariot of life, the author confronts two stark pathways at the brink of the financial collapse of his business: One path offers survival through strategic bankruptcy, steered by the mindset, "What's in it for me?"—a path rooted in self-preservation, expediency, and personal gain. The other path spirals into despair and resignation—the erosion of faith, purpose, and the soul's deeper calling.

Though opposite in appearance, both choices are rooted in the same illusion—the belief that life is either a battlefield to conquer or a pit into which one falls. Yet in the stillness between these extremes, a revolutionary choice emerges: Neither conquest nor collapse is embraced.

Instead, the sacred middle path of Oneness is chosen—a living state where positive and negative forces are not adversaries, but complementary expressions of a larger divine whole, held together in dynamic, conscious balance. By surrendering the personal will to the universal current of service, unity, and higher truth, the soul transforms not only its outer destiny, but its very relationship to existence itself. The business is not merely saved—it is reborn through a new mindset: "What am I here to give?"

From this celestial rising, an enlightened enterprise emerges, built not on competition, fear, or survivalism, but on service, contribution, and awakened leadership. It becomes a living testament that true success is not domination of life's forces, but conscious participation in their sacred unity.

Thus, The Chariot's deepest lesson is revealed: True triumph lies not in overcoming the forces of life, but in mastering the self through conscious alignment with the eternal Oneness from which all things arise.

Sacred Parallel – The Chariot and Krishna's Divine Duty on the Battlefield

The Chariot is pulled by opposing forces—light and shadow, ego and spirit—and the Charioteer must align them to move forward. On the battlefield, Arjuna stands upon Krishna's Chariot, paralyzed between despair and action, self-interest and sacred duty.

Krishna teaches that mastery is not found by choosing one extreme over another, but by rising through the middle path—the path of divine duty—where the soul acts in harmony with universal law. Arjuna's triumph lies not in conquest, but in mastering himself—in choosing truth over illusion, service over self-interest, and the higher will over worldly desire.

Sacred Parallel – The Chariot and Guru Nanak's Teaching on Balance and Destiny

Guru Nanak speaks of navigating life through divine order—the eternal command that governs all creation: "Hukam rajaa-ee chalnaa Nanak likhiaa naal."—To walk in harmony with divine will is to walk in truth.

Like the Charioteer, the seeker must hold the reins between opposing desires, emotions, and duties—not through control, but through surrender to a higher rhythm. Guru Nanak reminds us that when we move in accordance with the sacred design, victory is not measured outwardly, but felt inwardly—as the quiet triumph of purpose, alignment, and celestial guidance over the noise of confusion.

The Chariot, then, becomes a sacred vehicle—not driven by ego, but steered by the soul's remembrance of its center. For in Oneness, true mastery begins.

Education must become such a chariot—not a race for domination, but a journey of alignment. It must teach students how to steer through life's polarities with inner stillness, conscious responsibility, and ethical discernment. In this sacred approach, learning becomes not a means of control, but a path of balance—where every lesson, like every turn of the wheel, leads the learner closer to their true direction.

Card 8. Strength
Chapter 8: The Path of Wisdom to Education

Strength reveals the paradox of true power—gentleness stronger than force, compassion fiercer than domination.

This chapter reimagines education as an inner act of courage—the silent triumph of heart over mind, patience over impatience, and wisdom over mere knowledge. True education does not inflate the intellect; it fortifies the spirit with resilience, with the quiet might to endure, uplift, and transform through the noble power of contribution.

Sacred Parallel – Strength and Krishna's Teaching on Inner Fortitude

Strength is the card of gentle power—of taming the beast not through domination, but through patience, trust, and grace.

Krishna tells Arjuna that true strength lies in equanimity—the unwavering steadiness amid gain and loss, praise and blame, success and failure. The warrior's greatness is not in his might, but in the calm resilience that rises from inner peace. He is not hardened by battle, but softened by wisdom.

In both Strength and Krishna's guidance, we see this eternal truth: Courage without compassion is incomplete—and wisdom without humility is hollow.

Education inspired by this vision of strength must cultivate not just intellect, but inner steadiness—teaching students to remain grounded amid praise or pressure. When equanimity is honored as deeply as achievement, learning becomes a path of quiet power, where action flows not from ego, but from clarity, purpose, and calm self-mastery.

Sacred Parallel – Strength and Guru Nanak's Teaching on Inner Courage

Guru Nanak affirms that the greatest strength lies not in domination, but in the mastery of the self. He declares: "Mannai maarag thak na paai."—Recognize as strong the one who walks the path without faltering.

This valor is not rooted in aggression, but in compassion—the quiet might to protect, to uplift, and to walk the path of truth even when it is hardest. Like the woman taming the lion in the Strength card, Nanak's true warrior is the one who subdues ego with love, who meets adversity with stillness, and who stands firm in service to the voiceless.

Education, then, must mirror this sacred strength—not as a system of control, but as a sanctuary of empowerment. It should forge resilience through inner clarity and cultivate courage through compassionate action. In such a space, students are not shaped to conquer others, but guided to master themselves—to stand with truth, uplift the voiceless, and lead with love.

Card 9. The Hermit

Chapter 9: Who Am I – The Path to Self-Knowledge

The Hermit carries the lantern of inner light—illuminating the sacred necessity of solitude and soul-searching.

Here, education turns inward: Beyond textbooks, beyond institutions, the true curriculum begins—the eternal inquiry, "Who am I?" This chapter invites the student to step away from the noise of the world and journey into the silence where the only true teacher waits—the soul itself, sparkling and ancient.

Sacred Parallel – The Hermit and Krishna's Revelation of the True Self

The Hermit walks alone, lantern in hand, ascending the inner path to seek a light no world can give.

So too does Krishna, amidst the chaos of Kurukshetra, urge Arjuna to look beyond body, title, and fleeting identity—to realize the Atman, the indwelling eternal Self, untouched by birth, death, or circumstance. As the Hermit climbs the mountain of silence, Arjuna too must step back from the din of battle and listen for the soul's quiet truth.

True self-knowledge is not isolation—it is illumination. It is the awakening of inner light in a world governed by shadows.

To teach from this place is to guide students inward—encouraging solitude not as escape, but as a sacred return to essence. When learners are given the space to reflect, question, and walk their own path, education becomes more than instruction—it becomes illumination. The lantern of the Hermit, like the voice of Krishna, lights the way not to information, but to revelation—where the student does not merely know more, but becomes more: a bearer of their own truth, anchored in the eternal Self.

Sacred Parallel – The Hermit and Guru Nanak's Revelation of the Inner Light

Guru Nanak sings: "Gav-ee-ai suni-ai man rakhee-ai bha-o"—Sing, listen, and let the Divine dwell within your heart.

His call, like the Hermit's quiet journey, is an invitation to turn inward—not in retreat, but in remembrance. He reminds us that the radiant light of truth is not found through empty ritual or worldly acclaim, but through deep listening and the attuned stillness of soul.

The Hermit's lantern becomes the symbol of this sacred inner fire—glowing not to guide others first, but to reveal the path within. And like the mystic wandering through the wilderness of spirit,

Nanak beckons each soul toward the sanctuary where the voice of the Beloved can finally be heard.

Education must honor this sacred solitude—not as withdrawal, but as return. It must guide students not merely toward outward mastery, but toward the eternal flame already flickering within the cathedral of their own consciousness.

Card 10. Wheel of Fortune
Chapter 10: The Profound Path of Service and Karma

The Wheel of Fortune turns the great cycles of destiny—unseen currents of cause and effect moving through all life.

This chapter unveils a sacred truth: Education must align with the deeper laws of service and karma, where every action, every offering, seeds future worlds. Students are not merely recipients of knowledge, but conscious participants in the celestial rhythm of creation— planting seeds of kindness, humility, and contribution that shape the destiny of generations unseen.

Sacred Parallel – The Wheel of Fortune and Krishna's Teaching on Karma

The Wheel spins ceaselessly—weaving together the invisible threads of gain and loss, joy and sorrow, ascent and descent. It reminds us that life does not move in straight lines but in sacred spirals, echoing the eternal rhythms of cause and consequence.

Krishna, standing in the still center of the battlefield, unveils to Arjuna the ancient law of Karma: that no action vanishes into silence, that every thought, every deed, every choice sends ripples through the unseen fabric of time. The present is sculpted by the chisels of the past; the future is born from the seeds sown in this moment.

The Wheel reminds both seeker and warrior that true power lies in conscious participation with the ever-turning dance of life.

To teach in alignment with this truth is to guide students into a deeper awareness of their own agency—to help them recognize that every thought, word, and deed weaves itself into the fabric of their becoming. Learning becomes more than the absorption of knowledge; it becomes the art of conscious participation in life's unfolding. When students begin to see themselves not as passive recipients of fate, but as co-creators of their path, education transforms. It becomes a living initiation—where every lesson is a seed, every choice a turning of the Wheel, and every moment an invitation to shape the future with wisdom and intention.

Sacred Parallel – The Wheel of Fortune and Guru Nanak's Revelation of Divine Order

Guru Nanak reveals that all things unfold within the Divine Will—the Cosmic Order that governs every cycle of creation, transformation, and return. He proclaims: "Hukmai andar sabh ko, bahar hukam na ko-ay"—All are within the Divine Command; none exists outside of it.

Destiny, he teaches, is not the product of blind fate, but of conscious action—karmic echoes that ripple across lifetimes. This aligns with the Wheel's eternal turning: we cannot stop the spin, but we can choose how we move with it. To live in service is to turn the Wheel with grace, not resistance.

In education, this calls us to teach not just information, but orientation—helping students recognize the law of cause and effect, the value of selfless contribution, and the wisdom of aligning their actions with a greater purpose. When learners understand their role in the turning of the wheel, life itself becomes their curriculum—and service, their sacred response.

Card 11. Justice

Chapter 11: Adding the Highest Value

Justice stands as the keeper of cosmic balance—weighing each soul's deeds upon the scales of truth, intention, and consequence.

This chapter reflects a turning point in the learner's evolution: where education is no longer driven by personal ambition or competitive gain, but by a higher purpose—the call to live with integrity, to serve with compassion, and to contribute meaningfully to the collective good. It invites us to see knowledge not as a possession, but as a responsibility—to be translated into action that uplifts, restores, and harmonizes.

Here, learning transcends the accumulation of facts and becomes a covenant with life itself: to add the highest value, to act in service of the whole, and to live anchored in ethical clarity. Knowledge alone is hollow; wisdom—embodied through just action, conscious offering, and the refinement of one's innate gifts—is its highest fulfillment.

Sacred Parallel – Justice and Krishna's Vision of Righteous Action

Justice reflects the soul's alignment with universal harmony—measuring not just deeds, but the spirit in which they are done.

Krishna reveals to Arjuna that true righteousness does not arise from personal ambition or mechanical duty alone, but from sacred alignment—the soul's attunement to its highest truth within the divine design. Right action, he teaches, is that which is performed without attachment to outcome, grounded in inner clarity, humility, and surrender. In this light, Justice is not about retribution or reward—it is the restoration of balance, the healing of dissonance, and the return to the rhythm of divine order.

Education must reflect this deeper justice—not merely producing competent individuals, but awakening conscious stewards of the greater good. It must guide students to discern their inner calling, refine their unique capacities, and offer their gifts not in isolation, but in service to the whole. Only then does knowledge transform into wisdom, and learning into sacred contribution.

Sacred Parallel – Justice and Guru Nanak's Vision of Divine Balance

Guru Nanak speaks of divine justice as balance rooted in truth, not in punishment. He says: "Karmi aapo aapni, kay nayray kay door"— By our actions, we determine how near or far we are from the Divine.

This affirms that true justice is not external judgment, but inner alignment. Each action either deepens our union with Truth or distances us from it. Righteousness is grounded in truthful living, fearless honesty, and acting with fairness toward all beings.

This is reflected in the image of the Justice card: a crowned figure holding a sword of discernment in one hand, and a scale in the other— the very icon of accountability, clarity, and karmic balance. It parallels the story where Guru Nanak taught the merchant Duni Chand the futility of material accumulation by giving him a needle and asking him to carry it into the afterlife. In another tale, Nanak balanced the accounts of a greedy merchant—showing that true wealth is not what one possesses, but what one gives in alignment with divine truth.

In the realm of education, this calls for more than intellectual rigor—it demands the cultivation of inner balance, ethical clarity, and fearless honesty. Students must be guided not merely to excel, but to discern rightly, act justly, and live truthfully. Learning becomes a sacred offering when rooted in fairness, humility, and service—where knowledge is not used to dominate, but to uplift; not to accumulate, but to align. In this way, education mirrors the divine scales of Justice—teaching that the true measure of a life is not what one gains, but how one gives, chooses, and stands in truth when it matters most.

Card 12. The Hanged Man
Chapter 12: Becoming the Ultimate Lifelong Learner

The Hanged Man embodies the sacred paradox—through surrender, true mastery is born.

This chapter calls for a deep inversion: To become a lifelong learner is not to grasp harder but to release more deeply. Growth arises not by clinging to old certainties but by hanging suspended in mystery, open to seeing the world—and the self—through a soul's awakened eyes, humility, and the spirit of self-betterment, all in service to the greater good.

Sacred Parallel – The Hanged Man and Krishna's Call to Sacred Surrender

The Hanged Man inverts the world—inviting us to see not through the striving eyes of ambition, but through the still, illumined lens of surrender. Suspended between earth and sky, he reveals that wisdom dawns not through force, but through relinquishment.

So too does Krishna, on the battlefield of Kurukshetra, call Arjuna into this sacred paradox. He teaches that true learning begins not with conquest, but with the dissolution of the illusion of separateness. When personal desires are willingly hung upon the sacred tree of sacrifice, the soul's inner sight is restored.

Surrender, in Krishna's vision, is not a sign of weakness—it is the soul's highest strength. For only when we release our clinging to outcomes, identities, and rewards can the veils part and reveal the boundless wisdom that dances just beyond the grasp of the mind.

In this sacred pause, where the world hangs upside-down, the eternal truth turns right-side up.

True learning, like sacred surrender, requires the courage to release the grasp for outcomes and let go of identities built on performance. Not all wisdom is born of striving; some of the deepest truths emerge in stillness, humility, and the quiet pause between actions. When students are invited to trust the unfolding of their own inner journey, learning transforms—no longer a race toward accumulation, but a revelation that arises from presence, patience, and the soul's quiet readiness to receive.

Sacred Parallel – The Hanged Man and Guru Nanak's Revelation of Humble Surrender

Guru Nanak affirms that wisdom is not attained through egoic striving, but through the sacred humility of surrender. He declares: "Nanak hukmai je bujhai ta houmai kahai na ko-ay"—One who understands Hukam (Divine Order) speaks not from ego.

In the Tarot, the Hanged Man hangs upside down from a tree—not in agony, but in serenity. His inverted posture symbolizes a conscious reversal of worldly values, a voluntary surrender of control in order to see with divine clarity. His halo glows not from conquest, but from stillness.

Like the Hanged Man, Guru Nanak invites us to abandon the illusion of control, to be turned inside out and upside down by grace, and to view life through the lens of spiritual humility. Learning, in this light, becomes not an assertion of self, but the dissolution of ego into truth.

Education, then, must honor this sacred inversion—creating spaces of reflection, pause, and reverence, where mastery is no longer the pursuit of accumulation, but the quiet return to divine alignment.

Card 13. Death

Chapter 13: Self-Alignment—Integrating Holistic Practices into Our Lives and Education

Death is the sacred threshold between endings and beginnings— the gateway where illusions are shed, and the soul is invited into deeper alignment with its true nature. It is not a finale, but a metamorphosis—the falling away of what no longer serves, so that something more whole, more luminous, may be born.

In this chapter, education itself is summoned to the fire of transformation. Outdated systems, fractured frameworks, and narrow definitions of success are laid to rest—making space for a new paradigm that honors the fullness of the human experience.

From these ashes arises a holistic vision: one that nourishes not only the intellect, but the body, the heart, the spirit.

Here, education becomes a sacred act of self-alignment—a journey that integrates mindfulness, movement, stillness, and service into the rhythm of learning. It teaches not only how to achieve, but how to become whole. For only when the old is released with reverence can the new emerge with purpose, clarity, and grace.

Sacred Parallel – Death and Krishna's Revelation of Transformation

Death is not annihilation—it is the sacred gate through which life sheds its worn garments and is reborn in deeper truth.

To Arjuna, trembling on the battlefield of loss, Krishna reveals that the soul is unborn, eternal, and indestructible. What dies is not the Self, but its temporary expressions—bodies, roles, identities, and attachments. True death, he teaches, is not the end of life, but the dissolution of illusion. It is the falling away of what is false, so the eternal may rise.

This divine unraveling is the essence of transformation. Just as a snake must shed its skin to grow, the soul must surrender outdated beliefs, fragmented habits, and egoic pursuits to move into fuller expression. Endings, though painful, are portals—and in walking through them with awareness, we awaken to our higher nature.

Death, in Krishna's wisdom, is not a darkness to be feared, but a threshold to be honored—a sacred rite of passage through which we remember what is indestructible, essential, and free.

Education, too, must become such a rite of passage—not a system of preservation, but a process of sacred release. It must invite students to courageously let go of outdated paradigms, false narratives, and limiting identities, so that a fuller, integrated self may emerge. In this light, learning becomes a cycle of conscious dying and rebirth—where what no longer serves is laid to rest, and the soul's true potential rises anew in wisdom, clarity, and wholeness.

Sacred Parallel – Death and Guru Nanak's Vision of Transcending False Identity

Guru Nanak teaches that true transformation does not come through destruction, but through awakening—the gentle, piercing light of truth that dissolves illusion from within. He affirms: "Suni-ai dukh paap ka naas"—By deep listening, pain and falsehood are dissolved.

In the Tarot, the Death card portrays a solemn skeleton standing tall, a banner in hand, as the sun hovers near the horizon—neither fully setting nor fully risen, signifying both an ending and a sacred beginning. Below lie two figures: a fallen crown, symbolizing the end of worldly dominance, and a figure bowed—perhaps in grief, perhaps in awe.

This mirrors Nanak's wisdom: the dismantling of illusion is not a loss, but a sacred passage. The soul cannot awaken while clinging to the mask of self-importance. Ego—the false identity born of separation—must fall before divine remembrance can rise.

Education, then, must offer more than information. It must guide the learner through the sacred threshold of unlearning—where pretension dissolves, and the soul's innate brilliance is given space to rise. In that soul-lit emergence, we do not become less—we become more.

Card 14. Temperance
Chapter 14: The Re-Alignment Habits

Temperance is the art of alchemy and balance—blending opposing forces into a higher whole.

This chapter reveals that true mastery arises not from excess, but from the sacred balance of habits. Daily rituals of integration— weaving together structure and spontaneity, intellect and intuition, effort and surrender—form the gentle riverbed through which the soul can flow wisely and well across the journey of life, continually understanding and embracing the sacred path of realignment.

Sacred Parallel – Temperance and Krishna's Teaching of Sacred Balance

Temperance is the sacred blending—the alchemy of opposites—where action and rest, mind and heart, effort and surrender flow together in rhythmic harmony.

Krishna, the divine charioteer, counsels Arjuna to walk the middle path—to neither renounce the world in ascetic withdrawal nor lose himself in its fleeting pleasures. He warns against the illusions born of excess and deprivation, and reveals that true mastery arises not from rejection, but from integration. The path of sacred harmony, he teaches, is one of inner alignment—where every thought, word, and action is tuned to the divine rhythm of life.

Temperance, like Krishna's wisdom, is the art of sacred moderation—where one does not merely know the path, but walks it with rhythm, grace, and continuity. It is a call to live as a vessel of balance—steady yet supple, disciplined yet inspired—holding life's opposites in conscious harmony.

Education, in this light, must become an instrument of integration—cultivating not just achievement, but alignment. It must nurture in students the capacity to balance intellect with intuition, ambition with humility, discipline with joy. Rather than pushing extremes, true education teaches the art of equilibrium—where the learner is not pulled apart by competing forces, but learns to harmonize them into a meaningful, sustainable whole.

Sacred Parallel – Temperance and Guru Nanak's Teaching of Spiritual Equilibrium

Guru Nanak spoke of Sahaj—the serene, balanced state of being that blossoms from deep alignment with divine order. He revealed its essence in the timeless words: "Sahajay sahaj oopjai, sahajay sabh banai"—From Sahaj arises Sahaj itself; through it, all is beautifully fashioned.

This sahaj is not passivity, but the fruit of deep inner mastery—the graceful ease that dawns through union with the Eternal. It is the meeting place of stillness and movement, of flame and flow, of strength and surrender.

In the Temperance card, an angel stands as the alchemist of opposites—pouring water from one chalice upon a lion, symbol of untamed will, while holding a flame above an eagle, emblem of vision and spirit. This is the soul's sacred integration—not through domination, but through harmony.

Education must become a vessel for this sacred balance—guiding students not merely to acquire knowledge, but to blend courage with compassion, effort with ease, flame with clarity. When students learn to live from inner harmony, they no longer swing between extremes—they walk the middle path, where brilliance flows naturally, and life becomes the art of divine equilibrium.

Card 15. The Devil

Chapter 15: The Psychology of the Universe

The Devil reveals the quiet chains that bind us—illusions spun from fear, ambition, unconscious conditioning, and inherited beliefs.

This chapter explores how education often mirrors these hidden forces: transactional systems, shallow measures of success, and societal programming that prioritizes performance over presence. Yet true liberation lies not in rebellion, but in remembrance. Through the ten Universal Laws, the soul is gently called back into sacred alignment—where education evolves from conformity into transformation.

Freedom begins when illusion dissolves—when we remember that the highest aim of learning is not accumulation, but awakening.

Sacred Parallel – The Devil and Krishna's Revelation of Maya (Illusion)

The Devil unveils the chains we forge for ourselves—ego, status, ambition, and insecurity.

Krishna reveals to Arjuna that Maya—the great illusion—binds the soul by cloaking the transient in the garments of permanence, by convincing us that we are separate, incomplete, or defined by worldly achievement. He teaches that the Self is neither the body nor the mind, but the eternal witness behind both—unchanging, undivided, and whole. What we chase in fear, we lose in truth; and what we surrender in faith, returns as freedom.

Like the Devil card, Krishna's wisdom does not offer escape, but clarity. It is the inner light that shatters illusion and reawakens the soul to its native sovereignty. True liberation is not in renouncing the world, but in seeing through it—and acting from the undistorted center of the Self.

True education must do more than inform the mind—it must liberate the soul from falsehood, awakening each student to the infinite truth of who they already are.

Sacred Parallel – The Devil and Guru Nanak's Call to Inner Freedom

Guru Nanak spoke of the soul's entrapment by haumai—the ego-centered illusion that separates us from truth. He declared: "Bhukhiaa bhukh na utree je banna puriaa bhaar."—The hunger of desire is never satisfied, even with countless worldly possessions.

In the Devil card, a man and woman appear bound by chains—yet the chains are loose, revealing that their bondage is chosen, not imposed. Likewise, Guru Nanak reveals that it is not the world that binds us, but the illusion of separation within. Like the Devil archetype, ego represents the inner shackles of false identity, craving, and fear.

Education, then, must not deepen our fixation on outer success, but illuminate the inner path. It must help dissolve the illusions that bind—awakening the learner to sacred self-remembrance, humility, and the eternal freedom born of conscious choice and divine will.

Card 16. The Tower
Chapter 16: Real Communication

The Tower strikes like lightning—shattering false structures, dissolving illusions, and tearing away the facades we once mistook for truth.

In this chapter, the brittle architecture of superficial dialogue—scripted pleasantries, performative listening, communication driven by fear or agenda—comes crashing down. What emerges from the rubble is not ruin, but revelation. In the sacred dust of collapsed pretenses, a new language begins to rise—one forged from vulnerability, authenticity, and the raw, unfiltered presence of soul meeting soul.

Real Communication is not about polished speech or persuasive technique. It is about resonance—the courage to speak from the heart and the humility to listen with the spirit. It is the alchemy through which true connection is restored, wounds are healed, and silence becomes sacred again.

Sacred Parallel – The Tower and Krishna's Destruction of False Perception

Like a divine jolt, the Tower collapses illusions that obstruct the soul's evolution.

Krishna delivers a similar shock to Arjuna—not with thunder, but with the piercing clarity of divine wisdom. On the battlefield of Kurukshetra, he dismantles Arjuna's inherited notions of identity, duty, and morality. What Arjuna once called righteousness, Krishna reveals as veiled attachment. What he believed to be compassion, Krishna unveils as fear masquerading as virtue.

Real communication—with the self, with others, and with the Eternal—begins only when illusion shatters, and the soul stands exposed before the flame of truth.

Both the Tower and Krishna's revelation are sacred ruptures—divine disruptions that break what is hollow so something real may be born. They do not signal destruction for its own sake, but a necessary clearing, a holy demolition that makes way for a foundation built on awakened perception, higher purpose, and fearless authenticity.

In the realm of learning, Krishna's teaching compels a shift—from mere accumulation of knowledge to the fearless dismantling of illusion. Education must dare to question the unquestioned, challenge the inherited, and disrupt the comfort of convention. It must invite students to examine the scaffolding of their thoughts and dismantle what is built on fear, imitation, or untruth.

Only when the inner Tower collapses can a truer foundation emerge—one built not on borrowed beliefs, but on awakened discernment, soul-aligned purpose, and unshakable authenticity.

Sacred Parallel – The Tower and Guru Nanak's Revelation of the Divine Word (Shabad)

In the Tower card, we see a lightning strike shatter a lofty structure, casting crowned figures from its heights—a symbol of the collapse of false foundations, rigid beliefs, and ego-constructed identities. The fire and fall are not punishments, but awakenings—divine disruptions that make room for truth to enter.

Likewise, Guru Nanak reveals that real transformation begins when illusion crumbles and the soul listens—not with the ears, but with the heart. "Suniai sidh peer sur naath."—By deep listening, one attains mastery, wisdom, and union. The divine Word (Shabad) is not sound alone, but a living frequency that cuts through superficiality and summons the soul into remembrance.

The Tower's collapse mirrors Nanak's inner revolution—a shattering of hollow rituals, borrowed beliefs, and surface communication. Shabad is the thunder within: it dismantles false knowledge so that the soul may awaken to what is eternal and real.

To teach in the spirit of Guru Nanak is to cultivate sacred listening—the kind that tunes into silence, depth, and the vibration of truth. Here, education becomes an act of inner attunement, guiding students to hear beyond the noise of opinions and into the essence of being.

It is not enough to master speech; one must become receptive to the Wordless Word. Only then does communication become communion, and learning transcend knowledge to become illumination.

Card 17. The Star

Chapter 17: Mastering the Written English Language in the Age of AI

The Star shines as a beacon of authentic hope, clarity, and soul-expression.

This chapter calls students back to the sacred craft of writing—an act not of mechanical reproduction, but of spiritual imprint. In an era dominated by artificial voices, true writing becomes a revolutionary light—a conscious act of preserving the soul's eternal radiance amidst a mechanized world.

Sacred Parallel – The Star and Krishna's Assurance of Inner Light

The Star is the light that remains after destruction—quiet, unwavering, and pure. It is the soul's glimmering memory of what was never lost.

To Arjuna, overwhelmed by despair, Krishna offers this same sacred assurance: that beneath the battlefield's chaos and beyond the illusion of loss, the soul is eternal, untouched by death or doubt. He reveals that every trial, every sorrow, is part of a greater unfolding—guided by a wisdom that surpasses the mind. The true Self, Krishna affirms, shines not from the approval of the world, but from within—a radiant essence born of stillness, truth, and surrender.

In a world increasingly eclipsed by artificial voices and digital noise, the Star calls us back to this inner radiance—to the authentic expression that flows not from algorithms, but from the depths of the soul.

True education must become an instrument of this remembrance. It must teach students not only how to write, but why to write—not merely to inform, but to illuminate. Every sentence must become an offering of presence, every paragraph a constellation of clarity and compassion—a living truth that no machine can imitate, and no time can erase.

Sacred Parallel – The Star and Guru Nanak's Illumination through Divine Name (Naam)

Guru Nanak reveals that the eternal light—the true Star—is found in Naam, the Divine Name, which dissolves inner darkness and reconnects the soul to its immortal origin. He proclaims, "Akhar naam akhar salaah."—Through the Word, we know the Naam.

In the Star card, we behold a solitary figure beneath a vast sky, pouring water upon the earth and into a pool—a symbol of renewal, purity, and divine guidance after chaos. So too does the Divine Name pour into the soul like sacred light, gently restoring balance after the storms of ego and illusion.

In a world flooded with artificial voices and fragmented identities, this remembrance anchors the seeker in eternal clarity. Just as the Star offers hope, healing, and celestial orientation to travelers of the night, Guru Nanak's wisdom invites us to live and speak as vibrant vessels of divine heritage.

For students, this means writing not merely to inform, but to embody presence—crafting words that carry light, truth, and soul-unity in an age longing for authentic connection.

Card 18. The Moon

Chapter 18: The Re-Alignment of Our Core Character

The Moon governs the realm of dreams, illusions, and the deep waters of the subconscious.

This chapter guides the seeker through inherited shadows—the unseen conditioning and ancestral imprints that subtly obscure the soul's light. Education must not merely instruct; it must become a sacred journey of realignment, helping students navigate these veiled inner landscapes and return to the divine remembrance of their original, resplendent design.

Sacred Parallel – The Moon and Krishna's Teaching on Delusion and Self-Mastery

The Moon casts its silver light across the subconscious—revealing not clarity, but mystery. It illuminates the dreamlike terrain where illusion and intuition dance, where fear disguises itself as truth, and shadows masquerade as self.

To Arjuna, caught between duty and doubt, Krishna unveils the deeper battle—not against the world, but within the mind. He teaches that the untrained mind is like a restless moonlit sea—tossed by waves of emotion, memory, and confusion. But the mind, when mastered, becomes the soul's most powerful ally—a serene reflector of divine wisdom.

Like The Moon, Krishna's guidance invites the seeker to journey through veils of delusion, inherited fears, and subconscious patterning—not to escape them, but to see through them. The path to self-mastery begins not with denial, but with courageous awareness: walking through the mists of uncertainty to rediscover the soul's original radiance.

True character is not what we show the world—it is who we are when all illusions fall away.

Education must help students navigate this inner landscape—teaching them not merely what to think, but how to see. It must guide them to recognize the difference between fear and truth, reaction and wisdom, projection and presence. Only through this inner discernment can learners move from confusion to clarity, and from conditioned self to conscious soul.

Sacred Parallel – The Moon and Guru Nanak's Teaching on Inner Shadows and Realignment

Guru Nanak explains that spiritual clarity arises not through outward pursuit, but through piercing the fog of illusion and returning to divine remembrance. He declares: "Asankh moorakh andh ghor."—Countless are the fools lost in utter darkness.

The Moon card depicts a surreal twilight—a liminal space between knowing and not-knowing, where ancestral patterns, fears, and dreams flicker like shadows on water. Its veiled light speaks to the subconscious—the silent architecture beneath our actions.

Guru Nanak calls the seeker to illuminate these hidden realms through remembrance (Simran) and truth (Sach). He teaches that unless we realign the inner world, outer clarity remains unreachable. Just as the Moon reflects the sun's hidden radiance, so too must education reflect the soul's hidden brilliance.

In learning, this becomes a sacred task: not merely the transmission of facts, but the realignment of the self. True education must guide students through their inner shadowlands—helping them transcend inherited illusions and rediscover their innate clarity, dignity, and divine wholeness.

Card 19. The Sun

Chapter 19: The State of Modern Worldly Education

The Sun bursts forth with truth, joy, and clarity—revealing all that was hidden.

Here, modern education is seen with fearless eyes—its beauty, its brokenness, its latent possibility. Rather than condemning, this chapter illuminates the path forward: An education system reborn through authenticity, creativity, wonder, and reverence for the inherent brilliance within every soul.

Sacred Parallel – The Sun and Krishna's Revelation of Divine Truth

The Sun rises in brilliance—illuminating the path with joy, insight, and the unwavering light of truth that dissolves all illusion.

Krishna, after unveiling the soul's journey and the illusions of ego, reveals his cosmic form to Arjuna—an overwhelming, radiant vision of the eternal Self and the universal order. The Sun symbolizes this moment of full awakening: when the seeker no longer fears truth, but celebrates it.

The Sun reminds us to build systems that honor the brilliance within each soul—where joy, creativity, and purpose are not outcomes, but origins. It calls educators to cultivate environments of illumination—where students are not molded, but revealed; not judged by their shadows, but encouraged to shine. Learning, in this light, becomes an act of liberation—a sacred unveiling of the radiant essence that each student already carries within.

Sacred Parallel – The Sun and Guru Nanak's Teaching on Inner Radiance

Guru Nanak reveals that each soul carries within it the undying spark of the Divine—a radiant light untouched by shadow. He proclaims: "Ik Onkar Sat Naam, Karta Purakh, Nirbhau, Nirvair."—The One Reality is the eternal Truth, the Creator pervading all, fearless and without enmity.

This is not merely reunion—it is remembrance. The Sun card reflects this radiant awakening: a boy and girl stand together, hand in hand, beneath the brilliance of a golden sun, symbolizing innocence reclaimed, illusions dissolved, and truth fully illumined.

In the same way, Guru Nanak invites every seeker to shed the coverings of ego and ignorance, and to live in the fearless brilliance of Ik Onkar—the divine unity of Oneness pulsing through all existence. The one who recognizes this inner radiance walks not in doubt, but in joy, truth, and divine clarity.

For educators, this becomes a sacred task: not merely the cultivation of intellect, but the awakening of light—guiding each student to uncover their divine spark, and to shine that brilliance into the world with wisdom, courage, and compassion. Schools must become sanctuaries of enlightenment, where every child's radiance is seen, nurtured, and celebrated—so that education becomes not the acquisition of facts, but the unfolding of inner suns.

Card 20. Judgement

Chapter 20: What Makes a Lifelong, Highest-Value-Adding Student

Judgement sounds the sacred trumpet—calling the soul to rise, to remember, and to serve.

This chapter declares that education is no longer merely an individual pursuit but a communal resurrection: Students, parents, and teachers alike are summoned into conscious awakening and the divine interconnectedness of all life. The true measure of learning is not achievement, but contribution—the discovery of one's identity, uniqueness, and purpose through the living remembrance of our divine kinship.

Sacred Parallel – Judgement and Krishna's Final Summons to Sacred Duty

Judgement is the call to rise—not just as an individual, but as a soul returning to its sacred purpose.

Krishna's final message to Arjuna resounds like a cosmic trumpet: "Surrender all attachments. Act with devotion and trust in the higher order, and you shall find liberation." It is a call to release ego-driven striving and awaken to selfless, soul-aligned action.

In education, this is the moment students, teachers, and parents alike rise into conscious responsibility—guided not by reward, but by remembrance of their shared sacred origin. Schools must become spaces of moral awakening—where learning is not an escape from the world, but a deeper entrance into service and self-discovery.

Sacred Parallel – Judgement and Guru Nanak's Call to Inner Resurrection

Guru Nanak affirms that true life begins when we awaken from the slumber of illusion and ego. He proclaims: "Karmee karmee ho-ay veechar, sachaa aap sachaa darbaar."—By our deeds the soul is judged; the True One presides in the Eternal Court.

The Judgement card depicts a man, woman, and child rising from graves, arms lifted to the heavens, summoned by a celestial trumpet—symbolizing a sacred rebirth, a rising not to return to the past, but into divine purpose and higher awareness.

Likewise, Guru Nanak reveals that the true student is one who becomes attuned to the Teacher within, ever listening to the divine song of Oneness that calls the soul home.

For students, teachers, and parents, this marks the moment of inner resurrection—where learning is no longer a pursuit of personal gain, but a sacred contribution. Where knowledge ripens into wisdom, and identity dissolves into service. It is the flowering of the soul into conscious responsibility—a life lived not for the self, but from the

Self. Education, in this light, must become a vehicle for awakening—cultivating communities where learning is synonymous with ethical action and remembrance of one's highest nature.

Card 21. The World
Chapter 21: A Futuristic Transformative Vision of Education

The World completes the Fool's spiral journey—returning in unity, in mastery, in sacred wholeness.

This vision is no longer a distant dream; it is being lived and realized through places like Healthy-Mind International School—a sanctuary where the old paradigms of fear-based education have been dissolved, and a new paradigm rooted in love, purpose, and wholeness has begun to blossom.

Now, education is no longer confined to rigid textbooks or standardized tests; it becomes a dynamic unfolding of each child's innate potential, honoring the emotional, intellectual, and spiritual dimensions of growth. Students are no longer shaped into replicas of the past, but are nurtured as conscious creators of a new future—architects of destiny, taught not merely to succeed, but to serve, to wonder, to love, and to lead.

Sacred Parallel – The World and Krishna's Vision of Enlightened Unity

The World signifies sacred completion—the culmination of a soul's journey through illusion, shadow, surrender, and self-realization. It is the dance of one who no longer resists the flow of life, but moves in harmony with the divine rhythm that pulses through all things.

Krishna reveals this very state to Arjuna: the one who acts without attachment, aligned with their higher calling, transcends the dualities of gain and loss, pleasure and pain. Such a soul does not merely endure existence—they dance in freedom, interwoven with the eternal fabric of the cosmos.

Likewise, The World invites us into an education where knowledge is not fragmented, but whole—where mind, heart, and spirit flow as one. Learning is no longer a means to an end, but the living expression of unity itself.

Here, education becomes a sacred ecosystem—not driven by fear or division, but guided by balance, purpose, and joy. It is not the conclusion of a journey, but the revelation of its deepest meaning: that we were never separate to begin with.

Sacred Parallel – The World and Guru Nanak's Revelation of Wholeness in Unity

Guru Nanak sings: "Jin kau nadar karam tin kaar."—Through Divine Grace, the great harmony is realized; the soul returns to its wholeness.

With these words, Nanak affirms the sacred Oneness that underlies all creation—a divine kinship that transcends caste, creed, and culture. It is not sameness, but sacred interconnection: a cosmic family woven from the same thread of Light. His call is clear—to dissolve illusionary divisions and awaken to the living unity that pulses through all beings.

In The World card, a celestial figure dances at the heart of a green laurel wreath—the emblem of sacred completion and eternal victory. Surrounding her are the four living emblems: the man, the eagle, the bull, and the lion—guardians of the elements, symbols of the fixed zodiac, and archetypes of integrated being. Earth, air, fire, and water—body, mind, will, and spirit—no longer compete, but cohere in celestial balance.

The World mirrors Nanak's revelation of a life in alignment with divine unity—where the seeker becomes the light, the learner becomes the teacher, and the soul becomes the song.

In education, this final revelation is not an ending, but a sacred culmination—where learning dissolves the boundaries between giver and receiver, subject and self. It becomes a celebration of wholeness, a luminous dance of knowledge and compassion, of purpose and joy. Students do not merely graduate; they emerge as radiant co-creators—embodying harmony, living truth, and carrying forth the sacred rhythm of Oneness into the world.

0 (again). The Fool Returns
Chapter 22: Coming Full Circle

The Fool returns, no longer naive, but illuminated.

Having journeyed through illusions, trials, transformations, and sacred reckonings, the soul stands once again at the edge of the unknown—but now with eyes wide open, heart ablaze with purpose, and spirit radiant with wisdom.

No longer asking, "What must I learn to survive?" the awakened Fool now lives the higher question: "What am I here to give?"

In the vision realized through these reimagined educational models, the Fool's return is not merely symbolic—it becomes a living reality. It is the re-emergence of education as a sacred journey of becoming, where learning is not the filling of vessels but the awakening of souls. It is the celebration of education's true purpose—to ignite service, to birth wisdom, to nurture love, and to forge shining beings who carry the light of a new world.

The Fool has not merely acquired knowledge. He has become knowledge itself—a living testimony to the eternal truth: that the journey of learning never ends. It only deepens, expands, and ascends—forever.

Thus, the circle becomes the spiral, and the seeker becomes the light.

Sacred Parallel – Arjuna, Reborn as a Warrior of Light

Arjuna, who once trembled on the battlefield, now lifts his bow with clarity, humility, and divine alignment. The journey is not over—it never ends—but the traveler is changed. Now, each step is taken not in confusion, but in service; not in fear, but in love.

The soul has not merely learned—it has become the Way.

Sacred Parallel – The Eternal Fool and Guru Nanak's Lifelong Seeker

The Fool, once a naive traveler, now returns as the eternal seeker—the soul who walks not with certainty, but with surrender; not to conquer, but to serve. The path, as illuminated by Guru Nanak's wisdom, is ever unfolding—guided not by destination, but by divine remembrance. He gave humanity a spiritual compass in his utterance of Ik Onkaar—a revelation that could point anyone, from any path, back to the Oneness at the heart of all existence.

Through remembrance, service, and the divine word, the seeker finally reawakens to the cosmic unity—the soul-lit music that calls us all home.

Thus, the Fool's return mirrors the eternal seeker's path—a spiral of sacred humility, joyful discipline, and an iridescent flame of life offered as a song of the divine.

Summary Reflection

In "The Sins of Education," Card 0 The Fool—is the spirit of every seeker, every student, every teacher.

It represents:

The sacred promise at the beginning of the educational journey.
The awakening of innate potential.
The transformation through sacred trials,
And the ultimate rebirth into a life of conscious purpose, service, and unity.

Like the Fool stepping into the unknown, or Arjuna poised on his chariot, or the Sikh treading the eternal path, we begin in innocence—unsure, fragmented, searching. Yet through alignment with truth, sacred purpose, and inner wisdom, we return not to where we began, but to a higher octave of Self: illumined, integrated, fearless, and free.

The Fool's sacred number 0 reminds us:
Learning is not a destination, but an eternal becoming—a widening arc that draws the soul ever closer to its infinite home.

And thus, the journey comes full circle—not as an ending, but as a timeless beginning. For the education of the soul is not an ascent, but a return—a sacred homecoming to the indivisible whole.

About the Educators

Ratanjit S. Sondhe set foot on American soil in 1968, a young dreamer with little more than a few humble dollars in his pocket—and a heart full of faith in the sacred principle of Oneness: the belief that our highest calling is to infuse every endeavor with meaning, and to uplift the lives of all those we touch.

For over half a century, this unwavering purpose has been his compass, guiding him through a journey of extraordinary achievement. He founded and led the pioneering materials science enterprise POLY-CARB, Inc., which would later be acquired by The Dow Chemical Company in 2007—an emblem of success born not just of ambition, but of aligned intention.

Yet Ratanjit's legacy extends far beyond the boardroom. He is an enlightening voice—a visionary educator, author, lecturer, and radio and television host—whose words and broadcasts have transcended borders and touched hearts. With several books, award-winning papers, and more than 500 international broadcasts to his name, he has traveled the world, not to instruct, but to ignite inspiration—awakening minds and uplifting spirits wherever he goes.

His mission is a living mantra: to help souls rise into their truest selves—to succeed with integrity, reclaim their freedom, awaken their potential, and step boldly into a life of passion, purpose, and peace. A life not shackled by stress or limitation, but one that breathes the quiet joy of self-realization.

And the twin flame of this sacred work:

Gurdip Hari arrived on African soil in 1976, his heart and soul equally steeped in the divine principle of Oneness, and guided by a singular, selfless question: "What am I here to give?"

It was this enduring mindset that led him to success across many realms of life. But his true calling—his soul's deeper purpose—beckoned him to the realm of education, where he now pours his energy into transforming the global landscape of learning.

To give form to this vision, he founded Healthy Mind International School in Ghana—a lighthouse of wisdom and innovation, where ancient truths meet modern pedagogy. Here, education is not about the memorization of facts, but the awakening of spirit. It is a sacred process of nurturing each child's unique essence, allowing their innate gifts to rise, blossom, and shine.

At the heart of this movement is Gurdip Hari's pathbreaking work, published by Hay House—*The Mind is a Labyrinth with Three Keys: Unlock the Secrets of the Conscious, Unconscious and Super-Conscious.* Through its pages, he seeks not only to revolutionize education but to redefine its very meaning—illuminating a way forward where learning becomes a sacred journey of self-realization, purpose, and peace.